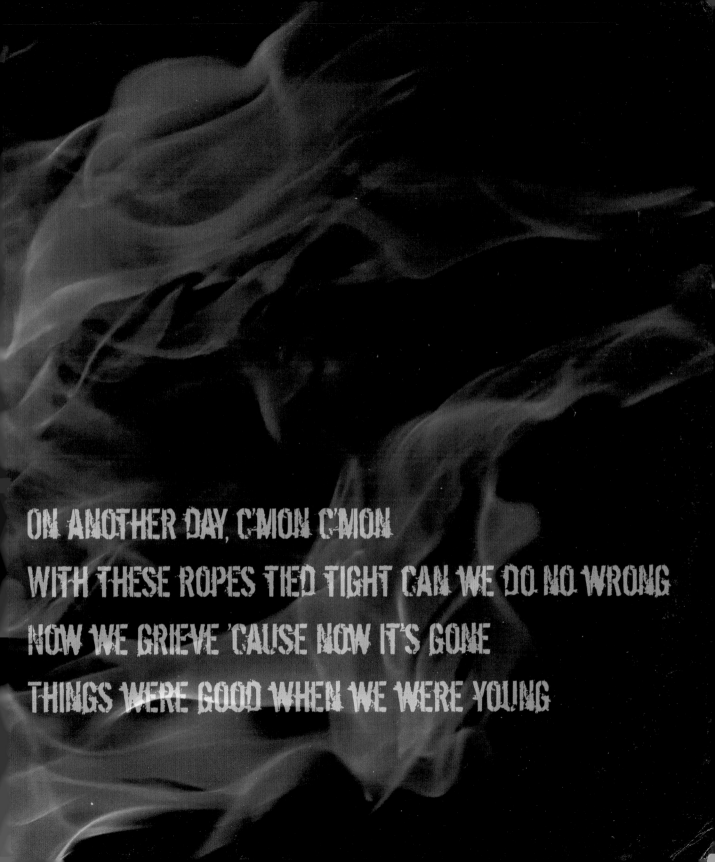

ON ANOTHER DAY, C'MON C'MON
WITH THESE ROPES TIED TIGHT CAN WE DO NO WRONG
NOW WE GRIEVE 'CAUSE NOW IT'S GONE
THINGS WERE GOOD WHEN WE WERE YOUNG

WITH MY TEETH BITE DOWN I CAN SEE THE BLOOD
OF A THOUSAND MEN WHO HAVE COME AND GONE
NOW WE GRIEVE 'CAUSE NOW IT'S GONE
THINGS WERE GOOD WHEN WE WERE YOUNG

IS IT SAFE TO SAY? (C'MON C'MON)
WAS IT RIGHT TO LEAVE? (C'MON C'MON)
WILL I EVER LEARN? (C'MON C'MON)

C'MON C'MON

AS I MAKE MY WAY – C'MON C'MON
THROUGH THESE BATTERED NIGHTS THAT SEEM TOO LON
NOW WE GRIEVE 'CAUSE NOW IT'S GONE
THINGS WERE GOOD WHEN WE WERE YOUNG . . . .

AND ON THIS DAY THESE DEEPENED WOUNDS
        DON'T HEAL SO FAST
CAN'T HEAR ME CROON
OF A MILLION LIES THAT SPEAK NO TRUTHS
OF A TIME GONE BY THAT NOW IS THROUGH

RESCUE ME

UNCENSORED

THE OFFICIAL COMPANION

"Rescue Me" Created by Denis Leary & Peter Tolan

Newmarket Press • New York

FIRST EDITION

10 9 8 7 6 5 4 3 2 1   10 9 8 7 6 5 4 3 2 1
ISBN: 978-1-55704-791-5 (paperback)   ISBN: 978-1-55704-792-2 (hardcover)

Library of Congress Catalog-in-Publication Data available upon request.

Quantity Purchases
Companies, professional groups, clubs, and other organizations may qualify for special terms when ordering quantities of this title. For information, write to Special Sales, Newmarket Press, 18 East 48th Street, New York, NY 10017; call (212) 832-3575 or 1-800-669-3903; FAX (212) 832-3629; or e-mail info@newmarketpress.com.

Website: www.newmarketpress.com

Manufactured in the United States of America.

Other Books in the Newmarket Shooting Script® Series Include:

About a Boy: The Shooting Script
Adaptation: The Shooting Script
American Beauty: The Shooting Script
A Beautiful Mind: The Shooting Script
The Birdcage: The Shooting Script
Black Hawk Down: The Shooting Script
Capote: The Shooting Script
The Constant Gardener: The Shooting Script
Dan in Real Life: The Shooting Script
Dead Man Walking: The Shooting Script
Eternal Sunshine of the Spotless Mind:
The Shooting Script

The Good Shepherd: The Shooting Script
Gosford Park: The Shooting Script
The Ice Storm: The Shooting Script
Juno: The Shooting Script
Knocked Up: The Shooting Script
Little Miss Sunshine: The Shooting Script
Little Children: The Shooting Script
Margot at the Wedding: The Shooting Script
The Matrix: The Shooting Script
Michael Clayton: The Shooting Script
The People vs. Larry Flynt: The Shooting Script
Pieces of April: The Shooting Script
Punch-Drunk Love: The Shooting Script

The Savages: The Shooting Script
Sense and Sensibility: The Shooting Script
The Shawshank Redemption: The Shooting Script
Sideways: The Shooting Script
The Squid and the Whale: The Shooting Script
Stranger Than Fiction: The Shooting Script
Traffic: The Shooting Script
Thank You for Smoking: The Shooting Script
Transamerica: The Shooting Script
United 93: The Shooting Script
War of the Worlds: The Shooting Script

Other Newmarket Pictorial Moviebooks and Newmarket Insider Film Books Include:

The Art of The Matrix*
The Art of X2*
The Art of X-Men: The Last Stand
Bram Stoker's Dracula: The Film and the Legend*
Chicago: The Movie and Lyrics*
Dances with Wolves: The Illustrated
Story of the Epic Film*
Dreamgirls

E.T. The Extra-Terrestrial: From Concept to Classic*
Gladiator: The Making of the Ridley Scott Epic Film
Good Night, and Good Luck: The Screenplay and
History Behind the Landmark Movie*
Hotel Rwanda: Bringing the True Story
of an African Hero to Film*
The Jaws Log
Memoirs of a Geisha: A Portrait of the Film

Ray: A Tribute to the Movie, the Music, and the Man*
Rush Hour 1, 2, 3: Lights, Camera, Action!
Saving Private Ryan: The Men,
The Mission, The Movie
Schindler's List: Images of the Steven Spielberg Film
Superbad: The Illustrated Moviebook*
Tim Burton's Corpse Bride: An Invitation
to the Wedding

CONTENTS

PREFACE

by Denis Leary*

*footnotes by Peter Tolan

SO HERE IT SITS.

Three pounds of paper and print.

Some of your favorite scenes. Many outstanding and arresting and visceral photographs.

Sean Garrity. Franco. Mike the Probie. Lou. Sheila. Not to mention Tommy, many other Gavins, and a good number of ghosts.[1]

A book full of faces and facts and arguments and snide remarks and sarcastic explanations and detailed sets of firehouse rules and infractions.

Discussions of life, love, sex, death, and everything in between. Especially food.

Page after page after page about the show that goes behind the scenes of 62 Truck.

Rescue Me *co-creators Peter Tolan and Denis Leary. Peter—shown here directing the pilot episode—is explaining to Denis how he wants more gravitas during the dramatic speech to the graduating class at the Fire Academy.*

All of us who work on *Rescue Me* are extremely proud of being able to make you laugh and then, one split hair of a nanosecond later, gasp. Or choke up. Or cry. Maintaining that high-wire balancing act is our greatest challenge in writing and performing scenes that deal with the issues facing firefighters today, whether it be lack of proper equipment or an argument over the racial and ethnic makeup of the department, or just a vicious kitchen spat about who drew a penis on the picture of Sean Garrity's mother (I, by the way, think it was Franco). Underneath all the drama and the pain and the fun, of course, lies the true underlying foundation of who they are and where they come from: September 11, 2001.

---

1. **Hello. Peter Tolan here. I'm doing the footnotes for this preface. I don't have a comment about the specific line indicated above. I'm just making sure this works. Yeah, I think it's fine. Sorry. Go back up and keep reading.**

PREFACE

The events of that day and the grief these men carry with them because of it speak to all of their actions: running into a burning building to save some poor soul; returning to the firehouse and discussing what went right and what went wrong while saving that poor soul so the next time the alarm sounds, they will be even better prepared as a team; arguing over who snuck the last slice of pizza while the aforementioned facts were being analyzed.

We take pride in presenting a full, complicated picture of a New York City firehouse in the days, weeks, and years following its biggest rescue. Because this is what gets lost in the smoke and anger and death of 9/11: It was the single greatest rescue in the history of the fire service. We know that 2,750 people perished in the Twin Towers. But we will never know how many thousands of people were saved by the actions of 343 of the FDNY's Bravest that awful morning.

So we set out to show you what makes a firefighter tick—in the firehouse, at home, at work, at play. The good, the bad, and everything in between. Complicated men doing a very complicated job.

It's hard to believe that this show almost never existed.[2]

In the fall of 1999, my business partner Jim Serpico and I, through our television and film production company called Apostle, were developing a television series based on the life and times of a friend of ours named Mike Charles. Mike was a detective with the NYPD for many years, and had been my technical consultant when I played a detective in *The Thomas Crown Affair*, a remake of the Steve McQueen/Faye Dunaway film from the late sixties, this time co-starring myself, Pierce Brosnan, and the absolutely delicious Rene Russo. (It's a terrific film directed by a terrific director named John McTiernan. You should rent it—or better yet, buy it.)[3]

I'd co-written scripts for several movies of mine, including one the director Ted Demme and I

---

2. You know, I've been reading up about footnotes to prepare for this. Did you know they're most often used as an alternative to long explanatory notes that can be distracting to readers? I can understand how a long explanatory note could be distracting. I mean, come on! Nobody likes to read in the first place, and then you've got these long explanatory notes all over the place! When I'm reading something, I don't want to be distracted. Enough said.

3. Yes, buy *The Thomas Crown Affair*, if only to see the haircut Denis wears in the thing. It's perfect for the character, but he could have worn a goddamn colander on his head and looked better. Let's put it this way: a mullet would have been a step up. What, the guy didn't have a mirror in his trailer?

made called *Monument Ave.*,[4] the ultimate Boston Irish gangster film (many critics have backed me up on that, so if you haven't seen it, go rent a copy right now—or better yet, buy a copy), but having never written a television script, I was seeking an experienced television writer to take the controls and show me the way. Someone[5] mentioned that Peter Tolan was available. Peter was the Emmy-winning partner of Garry Shandling on HBO's *The Larry Sanders Show*, which was not only still on the air but one of my all-time favorites.[6]

Tolan was interested, so a meeting was arranged at my farm in Connecticut. At that time, my wife, Ann, and I had about seventeen dogs. I'm kidding—we only had four. But it seemed like seventeen because two of them were Irish Wolfhounds. Huge Irish Wolfhounds. Let me qualify that—Irish Wolfhounds are supposed to be the largest dogs on the planet. We had two of the largest largest dogs on the planet. And one was actually retarded. Or a bear. We could never figure out which. His name was Duffy and he loved three things: food, sleep, and smelling peoples' crotches. Oh—and slobbering. So four things, really. But it was the crotch smelling and slobbering combo that Tolan was treated to within seconds of his arrival at the farm.[7]

After tossing some raw beef in Duffy's direction and pulling Clancy, the other Wolfhound, away from Peter's general direction, he and I sat and joked and laughed and ate and talked and dried off. Turns out we had almost the exact same background: he was born in Scituate, Massachusetts; I was born and raised in Worcester, Mass. He was of Irish descent; I was a first-generation Irish American.

4. Okay, compared to the haircut Denis wears in *this* film, the haircut in *Thomas Crown* looks like a Vidal Sassoon wet dream. You don't believe me? Buy a copy. Better yet, send me ten bucks and a stamped, self-addressed envelope and I'll mail you a copy. I've been working with Leary for almost eight years. Every birthday, every Christmas—another goddamn copy of *Monument Ave.* You know what? Five bucks. Make it five and I'll pay the postage.

5. If I ever find out who *this* asshole was...

6. Speaking of *Sanders*, the DVD collection *The Best of the Larry Sanders Show* is in stores now. Hey, if Leary gets to plug his stuff, I get to plug mine.

7. True story. Duffy was monstrously large and he had his cinder block of a head in my lap before I could even get out of the car. It was terrifying at the time, but I've been married for many years, so now I look back at my undercarriage getting that kind of attention with great fondness. Rest in peace, Duff. You're missed.

PREFACE

Denis explains to Peter Tolan and producer Jim Serpico that he doesn't know what the word "gravitas" means.

The initial signs looked good, so I gave him several pages of the pilot episode of this cop show that I had written.[8] His eyes glazed over the way most writers' eyes do when an actor says, "I've written some pages," but he took them, stumbled outside into the waiting tongue of Duffy, and drove off into the night.

Between the slobber stains and the pages, I half expected never to hear from him again. But to my surprise, he called back the next day to say he thought the pages were good and he thought we might have something here. Peter went to work writing the pilot episode for a half-hour single-camera sitcom about New York City cops. Things were looking very promising. Then my cousin Jerry died in a fire.

Jerry Lucey had always dreamed of becoming a firefighter. He got his wish when the Worcester Fire Department hired him. He quickly became one of its top rescue men, working out of a busy house in the downtown section of the city. On the night of December 9, 1999, an old cold-storage warehouse building caught fire when a homeless couple trying to keep warm lit a few candles. The candles caught some nearby newspaper, and Jerry and six other men died when the warehouse turned into an inferno. At the time it was the greatest tragedy in the fire service in a quarter of a century. My cousin's obituary—he was thirty-eight on the night he gave his life—called him a firefighter's firefighter. The ultimate compliment.

After endless days of searching for the bodies and watching firemen from all over the world arrive and put on their gear and climb into the burning, smoky remains of the building—after the six wakes and the six funerals—some form of supposedly normal life went on. The memories of my cousin Jerry were many. He and his firehouse crew worked every fall on an annual comedy benefit I hosted for my

8. An actor with pages is like a four-year-old with a Glock. Nothing good can come of it.

old friend Cam Neely's Cancer Fund. Cam was well on his way to the Hockey Hall of Fame and was still playing for the Boston Bruins—our favorite team since we were kids—so hanging around with Cam was something Jerry never really got over. To Jerry and his firehouse crew, Cam was a hero. In Cam's mind, the exact opposite was true.

Sometime after Christmas, I was getting ready to start work on a new movie called *Double Whammy*. (It's a funny, quirky little indie co-starring myself, Steve Buscemi, and the absolutely luscious Elizabeth Hurley. It was directed by the incredibly talented Tom DiCillo, and you should treat yourself to a copy when you pick up *Monument Ave.* and *The Thomas Crown Affair*.)[9] Tolan's script came in. Needless to say, it was brilliant.[10] We thought our twisted, dark comedy would be a perfect fit for cable, but some months later found ourselves pitching at ABC, after they had expressed interest. Peter and I went in with a very basic pitch to the ABC execs: *You are not going to want to do this show.* It's too dark, too expensive (the show had to be done in New York City), too filthy, too everything you will never put on the air. "Forget we were ever even here," we told them. Naturally, they bought it.

Peter and I set about writing the first thirteen episodes of quite possibly the darkest situation comedy ever seen on network television. Meanwhile I was making *Double Whammy*—and between setups, found myself jotting down ideas for a story about a firefighter. One who dies in the line of duty. Summing up his life in two hours' time. His wife and kids. The guys he works with. And unlike most overblown, completely unrealistic Hollywood treatments of the firefighter's world, I decided I was going to make a film firefighters would find true, right down to every technical and emotional detail.

The Leary/Tolan cop show, *The Job*, went on air in the spring of 2001 and was an immediate critical success. One critic went so far as to call it the best half-hour since *I Love Lucy*.[11] It was dark, edgy, and really, really funny. (If you missed it, pick up *The Job* box set when you're out buying *Monument Ave.* and *The Thomas Crown Affair*. Oh, and pick up *Ice Age* and *Ice Age 2* while you're at

9. Okay, I've just been poking around here and I've got, like, twenty copies of *Monument Ave.* and sixteen copies of *Double Whammy*. I'll go ten bucks for both, postage paid. Christ, come on! Like you're going to find a better deal!
10. $7.50 for both. Final offer.
11. Ann Leary, *The Southern Connecticut Equestrian Monthly*, Late Summer/Fall Issue 2000, pp. 12-14.

PREFACE

it—my kids are going to college this year and it's going to be pretty goddamn expensive.) The show was truly one of a kind. Naturally, ABC had absolutely no idea what to do with it. We had supporters at the network, but a new entertainment president came in—a woman who shall remain nameless [12]—and she was not a fan. The show was picked up for a second season, but just barely. We set about shooting the second season of *The Job*, to debut in the fall of 2001. But that September 11th, everything changed.

John Scurti explains to Mike Lombardi (seated) that Gravitas *was not a techno band from the late eighties as Peter and Denis listen in.*

To say the least.

There are people who panic and run and hide and cry in response to almost any crisis. Ninety-five percent of them work in network television.

ABC's reaction was to put all comedy in an indefinite holding pattern. Our air dates disappeared. Production shut down. We heard that the country was no longer in the mood to laugh, and especially not at a warts-and-all depiction of the life of a New York City public servant. (Of course, this was bullshit. I did my Cam Neely benefit gig a few weeks after 9/11. The crowd of 5,000 not only shook the building with laughter, but gave us a standing ovation after we spent a few hours pissing all over terrorists, new air travel regulations, and that asshole bin Laden.) *The Job* stayed off the air until the following spring. Our audience found us again after a second wave of insanely great reviews. I was in London when the show premiered there to reviews like "The best American import since *Seinfeld* and *The Sopranos*." Naturally, ABC canceled us.

Extremely disappointed, I went back to working on my firefighter idea, and took an acting job in

12. Susan Lyne, ABC Entertainment President from January 2002 to May 2004. Other information available at tolanholdsagrudge.com. Twenty-five-dollar membership fee gets you coupons for one dozen eggs, a six-roll pack of Charmin Ultra, and Ms. Lyne's home address.

another movie, *The Secret Life of Dentists*. (A fantastic film, co-starring me, Campbell Scott, and Hope Davis, and directed by Alan Rudolph. Add it to your list of purchases. By now you're probably eligible for free shipping through amazon.com.) I spent a lot of time reading and/or hearing about articles from all over the country talking about how great *The Job* had been, and getting calls from former cast members who were in meetings in Los Angeles where producers were all saying how they wished they could make a show like *The Job*. Somewhere in the middle of all this, Peter and I started talking about doing something new together, but not for network television. I remember it being Peter (but he remembers it being me) **13** who came up with the brilliant idea of not making my firefighter idea a movie, but instead making a dramatic series about the real-life world of a New York City firehouse and the men who work there. The more we talked about it and the more I sat around staring at my notes for the movie, the more I fell in love with the idea.

I took Peter to Terry Quinn's firehouse—it was the one I was most familiar with in the city, and it happened to be in the neighborhood Ann and I had lived with the kids for many years. Peter got to meet all the guys on Terry's crew, and we rode along on a couple of calls. I'll never forget the look on Peter's face as we raced to a fire in the chief's Suburban. We were probably doing about 110 with the chief talking calmly over his shoulder as the driver deftly wove in and out of traffic, easily avoiding several collisions. One night we caught a call at a Chinese restaurant. All the guys ran in, and Peter and I stayed outside with the chief. A news truck pulled up and one of the reporters, looking at the restaurant in question, asked the chief if there were any Chinese firefighters. "Yeah, I'm sure there are," he said, giving her a sharp look. "Somewhere over in fucking China." That line made it into one of the first episodes of what became known as *Rescue Me*.

Peter and I worked for several weeks writing the pilot episode—each writing separately and then switching off pages and rewriting each other—until we were both happy with the finished product: a

---

13. No, I remember it being me, too. Yeah, *Rescue Me* was all my idea. I can recall the exact day I thought it up. I was in the city soon after 9/11, and I was talking to Denis, and we were watching firefighters from all over the country rushing down to the site, working for hours on end without sleep, and Denis said to me, "You know, *The Job* is great, but this—the story of these guys—*this* is the show we should be doing."

Shit. Forget it.

PREFACE

realistic, unusual blend of intense drama and balls-out comedy. It was a tough mix—and a tough sell—but pretty soon all the broadcast networks were calling Jim Serpico asking to see the script. The answer to everyone was no. We'd learned our lesson with *The Job*: Cable was the way to go. HBO got hold of it and wondered whether they could buy the rights. The answer was no. USA Network called and said they would guarantee us thirteen episodes on the air and a huge budget—but we'd have to shoot in Toronto. A very loud no. HBO called back and asked if it could be done as a half-hour comedy. The same answer, louder. USA called back and said we could film the exteriors in New York City and the rest in Toronto. HBO called back a third time to talk with me directly. All I heard were the words "There are some very interesting things in this script, but we were wondering. . . ," and then my cell phone cut out. I decided not to call them back.

The next day Kevin Reilly and Peter Liguori called from FX. They loved the *Rescue Me* script, but they had some notes. I started to hang up, but before I could, I heard one of the notes and it was actually smart and informed and helpful. Tolan and I were impressed with the notes, not to mention the fact that they laid out their marketing plan—when and where and how much they would spend on advertising (which no network ever tells you, especially before you're in business with them)—and by the great job they'd done with their first dramatic series, *The Shield*. We signed on and started looking for a cast.

The part of Kenny "Lou" Shea we had written with John Scurti in mind.[14] John and I worked opposite each other in Ted Demme's *The Ref* (I'm starting to feel guilty about all these movies you have to buy—have you considered Netflix?), the classic anti-Xmas comedy starring myself, a very funny Kevin Spacey, and the always great Judy Davis. Scurti and I became fast friends, and I used him in a mockumentary of reality shows Apostle did for Comedy Central called *Contest Searchlight*. (It's not available on DVD. You caught a break.) Mike Lombardi came from that same production, where he

---

14. Denis says we had Scurti in mind for Lou, but the fact is I'd never even *met* John before he was cast. I was extremely apprehensive about casting someone I didn't know, and Denis was protective of John and pretty much told FX, "He's my guy and he's getting the part." It could have gone wrong about a million different ways, but Scurti turned out to be pure gold. I can put the hardest joke in his mouth and he rolls it out like silken honey. As I tell John at least twice a season, he's one of the most watchable actors I've ever worked with.

played a wide-eyed newcomer to show business and the big city. The role of the probie didn't seem like too much of a stretch. [15]

We had always pictured the part of Chief Jerry Reilly being played by Lenny Clarke, who was so brilliant on *The Job*. Lenny and I are friends from way back, and I used him in the movies *Monument Ave.* (pick up a couple of copies—it makes a great gift) and *Two If by Sea* (pick up a couple of copies and destroy them—it blows). Unfortunately, Lenny was doing a network show and making good money—it's all about the goddamn money with Lenny, the goddamn whore—so he was unavailable. Fortunately, he called an actor buddy and told him about the role, and that actor buddy knew Tolan and called him at the Apostle offices, but they wrote

Director Jace Alexander explains to Denis that he not only saw Gravitas *live several times during the late eighties but was in fact their keyboard player during a 2003 reunion tour.*

down the wrong name on the message they gave Tolan, and Tolan got pissed off because whoever Dan McGee was, he had some nerve calling up pretending he knew him to get a foot in the door. Peter sat bolt upright in his hotel bed at eleven o'clock that night and said, "*Jack* McGee?" He called Jack—a former firefighter up in the Bronx, by the way—early the next morning, [16] an audition tape was sent to New York immediately, I watched it, gave the thumbs-up, and we had our Jerry Reilly.

The women were easy to find. Callie Thorne had auditioned for *The Job* several years earlier and

15. Mike also appeared in a small role in an episode of *The Job*. He played a sweet, shy, non-English-speaking pool boy at a Florida resort where Mike McNeil (Denis) took his girlfriend for a weekend vacation. I directed the episode and Lombardi was great, but that was the show we were shooting on the morning of September 11, 2001. I've never watched it.

16. It turned out to be *very* early. I was in New York and Jack was on vacation in Hawaii with his wife when I returned his call. I think it was 3:40 in the morning his time. Okay, it's not much of an anecdote. It's a footnote for a reason, asshole.

PREFACE

Charles Durning (center) contemplates punching Peter Tolan in the side of the head as Tatum O'Neal, Denis Leary, and Callie Thorne tell John Scurti (off camera) to stop eating all the birthday cake needed for an upcoming scene. Steven Pasquale—seated to Denis's right—is not only egging Peter Tolan on but patiently waiting for Durning to attack.

had come very close to winning the role that went to Diane Farr. We had a lot of great actresses interested in the role of Jimmy's widow, Sheila Keefe, but Callie came in and all the competition fell by the wayside. She was funny, quick, sexy—and there was a very subtle crazed look in her eyes that took the role places we'd never imagined. She was electric.

Peter went out to California to search for a Janet and called us just after Andrea Roth had left the room to say how fantastic she was. Hot, cold, hard, soft: She was everything we were looking for to play Tommy Gavin's wife.

Our great casting luck continued. For Tommy's cousin Jimmy Keefe, we went back to a terrific actor who played a guy who kind of looked like me on *The Job*: Jimmy McCaffrey. Lenny Clarke kept his amazing streak alive with yet another network flop, and came aboard late to play Uncle Teddy. Charles Durning [17]—whom I had worked with in the David Mamet film *Lakeboat*—agreed to play my dad. We called in Diane Farr—who had such perfect comic timing as *The Job*'s sole female detective, not to mention a great smile and the right energy—to play the new female firefighter in the house in our second season.

We had two major challenges in casting our regular guys: the parts of Franco Rivera and Sean Garrity. We looked at tapes and beat bushes and met every good-looking Hispanic or black actor around the age of thirty in the continental United States. No Franco. We saw hundreds of young guys for the role of Sean. None of them was right. We were coming down to the wire, and still those roles were uncast. Maybe we'd

17. I want to pause here and say two words: Charles Durning. Do you realize how lucky we were to have Charlie come aboard? We did, every single minute of every scene he did. An inspiring actor. A beautiful man. And the teller of some of the worst jokes you've ever heard in your life. We laughed at every one of them.

been too lucky with all the other roles. Maybe this was some weird form of casting karmic payback. And then, just as things were looking really goddamn bleak, Daniel Sunjata and Steven J. Pasquale walked into a casting session one right after the other. [18] Danny had been in the play *Take Me Out* on Broadway, and he had the immediate elements we were looking for in Franco: handsome, cocky, brown/black. Pasquale had also been working on the New York stage, but was primarily known for dramatic roles. Sean Garrity promised to be one of *the* funniest characters, if not the funniest, on the show. Steve had never been hired for comedy. Now that we all know what he can do, that's kind of amazing, isn't it?

We had our cast. Then came what's often the scariest part of putting a television show together: getting all the actors in the same room and seeing whether the chemistry is there. Which it was—in spades. All the faces and the comic timing and the various little tics and tremors and the inches of angst and the sexual tension—it was all there before, during, and after our first table read. Peter and I walked out of that room with big smiles creasing our Irish faces.

My son Jack found the Von Bondies song "C'mon C'mon" and mentioned it to me because he knew how hard I'd been trying to find something with the perfect feel for the opening of the show. Terry Quinn had taken the opening credits photo crew out and shot some firehouse footage and some traveling shots, and they had cut an opening sequence to a slow song. I hated it. I wanted something that made you feel like a fire alarm had just gone off and that *Rescue Me* was actually driving itself off the screen and into your living room. When Jack played "C'mon C'mon" for me, I knew it was exactly what we needed. John Landgraf, who had been recently named the new head of FX, felt there was no way we could cut our existing title footage into a new, harder-edged title sequence, but only a few days later we saw what you see each and every time you watch the show.

18. **I was the person in the room at the casting session where Danny and Steve first came to us. After they left, I breathed for maybe the first time in a month. My favorite casting story involves Olivia Crocicchia, who came in for (and got, as it turned out) the role of Katy Gavin. Olivia was quite young. She came in and sat down—her feet didn't even touch the floor. She was red-cheeked and adorable—a Hummel figurine come to life. I asked her what work she'd done recently. "I was on *Law and Order*," she squeaked. "Oh," I said. "What did you do on that?" She sat up and smiled proudly, showing a missing front tooth. "I was the victim of a pedophile!"**
   I love show business.

PREFACE

A few words about Landgraf: We love the guy. It's not often you hear creative types expressing anything other than outright hostility for television executives (go back and reread the ABC/*The Job* part of this preface), but John not only totally supports our show and lets us do whatever the hell we want, but on many occasions he's given us a note or a suggestion that makes us turn to each other and say, "Why the hell didn't we think of that?" John is and always has been a supreme fan of the show. He's one of the main reasons *Rescue Me* has flourished.

The show is not traditional in any sense of the word, and that carries over into how we produce it. A typical day[19] involves Peter and me and Evan Reilly (a fellow producer, our only other regular writer, and *Rescue Me*'s very talented secret weapon) discussing what we have to shoot that day, and making sometimes minor and sometimes sweeping changes, often over our cell phones while we're driving to work. When we get to set, we inform the actors that we're throwing some or most of the dialogue out the window, and we'll either be rewriting it while they go through makeup and hair or they'll be improvising around the original idea of the scene. There are many days when the scenes—comic or dramatic—are so delicately written and balanced that it's just a matter of running the lines and getting the rhythms right. And then there's the madness of the throw-the-shit-out-and-improvise days.

I'll tell you this: Almost every single day on the set of *Rescue Me* has been a thrilling experience. Yes, there are some long, boring, difficult and time-consuming scenes—any scene involving smoke and/or fire isn't going to go down without a fight. But on this show, the good/exciting days far outweigh the boring ones. More often than not, we're watching Callie surprise and amaze us with one scene while Sunjata, Scurti, Lombardi, and Pasquale are over on another set coming up with a newer, better, partially improvised version of the scene we are planning to shoot next. It is—in three, short little words—a goddamn blast.

Those fire scenes. They're often slugged into the script this way:

> EXT. MANHATTAN STREET - NIGHT
> 62 Truck screeches to a stop in front of a burning building. (For further instructions and dialogue, see Terry Quinn.)

---

19. **A typical day? On *Rescue Me*? No such thing, kids.**

We usually turn our fire scenes over to our technical adviser Terry Quinn, who still works as a real New York City fireman, and have him tell the actors what to do and what to say so it all looks authentic. He fills the trucks and the streets and the buildings with our extras—also all real firemen—and this is what gives our fire scenes the sense of realism they've become famous for. More than once or twice, real life has mirrored art in an extreme way. In season 3, I think, Evan, Peter, and I decided we wanted the crew to solve a burning-schoolbus rescue. I called Terry on his cell and floated the idea by him. "How do you think that would work?" I asked him. "I'll call you back with a couple ideas a little later," he said. "I'm pulling up to a burning bus right now." He hung up, jumped off the rig with his crew, put out the fire, and saved all the kids. Then he called us back and gave us a blow by blow—which is pretty much what we used in the scene.

We also rely heavily on our stuntmen and our stunt coordinator, Danny Aiello III. I believe in letting stuntmen earn their pay, so we use Danny's guys for anything and everything.[20] (Although I think you'll find that many of the more dangerous fire scenes from season 4 in particular used the actual actors in many of the stunts. The naked eye doesn't lie, so we hoped to up the ante and get you on the edge of your seats wondering how Leary and Scurti and Pasquale were falling through that floor or out that window or up that elevator shaft.)

If you bought this book, I'm going to assume you really love the show. I want you to know that as much fun as you have watching *Rescue Me*, we have at least ten times as much fun making it. It has been the single greatest experience of my professional career, and we all look forward to doing it over and over again for at least a couple of more years.[21] And maybe another book.

Read and enjoy.

And don't forget to blow out those candles.

20. It's a crazy business, but stuntmen and women—they're the ones out front holding the crazy banner. The simple reason? A good day for our stuntpeople is the day they almost die. If you didn't come close to killing yourself, you weren't really trying. I honestly worry about them—until we have to throw somebody off a building.
21. I second. Thanks, Denis—it's been a great ride so far. And thanks to our great cast, our above-and-beyond crew, and a post-production department that rises to every challenge we throw at them—and throw we do. More thanks to our support system at Sony Pictures Television and FX. You all deserve more than a footnote. So I'm sending you copies of *Monument Ave.* and *Double Whammy*. Don't worry—I'll eat the postage.

ROLL CALL

LADDER 62

DENIS LEARY
TOMMY GAVIN
*(controls the drinking and
the crazy hero stuff)*

MICHAEL LOMBARDI
MIKE "THE PROBIE" SILETTI
(in charge of the homo crap)

JACK McGEE
JERRY REILLY
(the Chief)

STEVEN PASQUALE
SEAN GARRITY
(controls the retard bullshit)

JOHN SCURTI
LT. KENNETH "LOU" SHEA
(poetry is his turf)

DANIEL SUNJATA
FRANCO RIVERA
(the pussy man)

GAVIN'S FAMILY

ANDREA ROTH
JANET GAVIN
(Tommy's wife)

CALLIE THORNE
SHEILA KEEFE
*(widow of Tommy's
cousin Jimmy)*

DEAN WINTERS
JOHNNY GAVIN
*(Tommy's brother, now
deceased)*

TATUM O'NEAL
MAGGIE GAVIN
(Tommy's sister)

LENNY CLARKE
TEDDY AKA THEODORE
(Tommy's uncle)

CHARLES DURNING
JOHN GAVIN, SR.
(Tommy's dad)

JAMES McCAFFREY
JIMMY KEEFE
*(Tommy's cousin, killed
9/11)*

JERRY ADLER
CHIEF FEINBERG

KATE BURTON
ROSE

LYNDON BYERS
RYAN

ROBERT JOHN BURKE
FATHER MICKEY GAVIN

ROLL CALL

NATALIE DISTLER
COLLEEN GAVIN

OLIVIA CROCICCHIA
KATY CAVIN

JENNIFER ESPOSITO
NONA

PATTI D'ARBANVILLE
ELLIE

PHIL ESPOSITO
IZZY

ROLL CALL

ADAM FERRARA
CHIEF "NEEDLES" NELSON

GINA GERSHON
VALERIE

MILENA GOVICH
CANDY

TREVOR HEINS
CONNOR GAVIN

ARTIE LANGE
KENNY'S COUSIN

ROLL CALL

SUSAN SARANDON
ALICIA

SUSAN MISNER
THERESA

SHERRIE SAUM
NATALIE

CAM NEELY
MUNGO

AMY SEDARIS
BETH

ROLL CALL

LEE TERGESON
SULLY

CAILIN STOLLAR
KEELA

MARISA TOMEI
ANGIE

LARENZ TATE
BLACK SEAN

CORNELL WOMACK
RICHARD

CHAPTER 1

THE JOB: TALKING ABOUT THE BITCH

I'M NO HERO, I'M A FIREMAN...

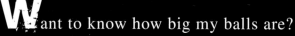

Want to know how big my balls are?

My balls are bigger than two of your heads duct taped together.

I've been in the middle of shit that would make you piss your pants right now. Uptown, downtown, Harlem, Brooklyn. But there ain't no medals on my chest, assholes. I'm no hero.

I'm a fireman.

We're not in the business of making heroes here, we're in the business of discovering cowards 'cause that's what you are if you can't take the heat. You are a pussy and there ain't no room for pussies in the FDNY. You pussies better pray you don't get assigned to my firehouse because I have seen it all.

I knew sixty men who gave their lives at ground zero. Sixty! Four of them from my house.

Vito Costello, found him almost whole.

Ricky Davis, found him almost whole, hugging a civilian woman.

Bobby Vincent found his head.

And my cousin Jimmy Keefe, my best friend. Know what they found of him? What they were able to bring back to give his parents? A finger; that's all. A finger. These 4 men were better human beings and better firefighters than any of you will ever be.

—**Tommy Gavin**

SO YOU WANT TO BE A FIREMAN?

TOMMY: Look — we get paid shit. We'll always get paid shit 'cause the politicians got us by the balls 'cause we never go on strike. Everybody respected us after 9/11 but this whole country's got A.D.D. so that's all water under the bridge and now we're back to being glorified garbagemen. Garbagemen with booze and drug problems.

Maybe I should take you over to the burn unit, let you see what you're always this close away from. Or let you ride the rig with us for a couple days so you can see the death — little kids whose charred lips get stuck to yours while you're giving them mouth to mouth — or babies — newborn babies — dead in their sleep 'cause the fire spread so quick — their backsides stuck to the melted mattress underneath 'em. The dead cats, the burnt puppies —

Listen — that's one side a the coin. The other? Ain't no job on this planet I'd rather do. Every day — every goddam day — you make a difference. Just like your old man did. The politicians? They ain't worthy to kiss the boots your old man died in.

DAMIEN: I know.

TOMMY: I came over here to talk you out of this but I can't do it. I know how you feel, Damien — this fire thing — it's in our family's blood. It's in our bones. Your Dad — if he was here — he'd never admit this — I think he'd want nothing more than to see you pick up his badge and carry on.

Tommy has pulled out his wallet and now he flips it open — it's Jimmy's badge.

DAMIEN: That's — my Dad's?

TOMMY: I've had it with me — in my wallet or in my bunker gear — every day since they buried him. They gave it to me to keep for you.

DAMIEN: Really?

TOMMY: Firefighter dies on the job — they retire his badge. No one else can have it. Except his son — if and when he decides to come on.

CODE OF THE FIREHOUSE

RULE 1 If you ain't scared, you're crazy.

RULE 2 When we have sex with women who are not our wives we make every detail available to other guys.

RULE 3 A lot of guys see widow banging as a breach of certain unwritten rules

MEET THE PROBIE

MIKE—the probie—enters. He's carrying
various vegetables. Cooking his first
meal for the crew. He tenses up when
he sees Tommy.

TOMMY: Jesus Christ — this is what
 they send us? What's your name, kid?

MIKE THE PROBIE: Mike?

TOMMY: You asking me or telling me?

MIKE THE PROBIE: It's Mike.

TOMMY: Well, that won't work. We got too
 many Mikes around here already.
 Irish Mike, Polish Mike. . .

SEAN: Mike the Mick.

LOU: Big Mike. Little Mike.

TOMMY: You Jewish?

MIKE THE PROBIE: No. Why?

TOMMY: Then you could be Mike The Kike.

MIKE THE PROBIE: I'm Italian.

SEAN: Forget it. There's already a Guinea Mike over on Ladder 12.

TOMMY: Not to mention Mike The Wop over on the Upper East Side.

LOU: You know what? Screw it. New Mike.

TOMMY: New Mike it is.

MIKE THE PROBIE: But — what if I'm here for, like, ten years —

TOMMY: Well, I don't think that's gonna be a problem, kid. Don't worry about it. Hey, New Mike, get me a coffee.

FIRST HIGHWAY CALL

INT. FIREHOUSE/TRUCK AREA — NIGHT

FRANCO: First West Side Highway call, kid?

MIKE THE PROBIE: Yeah.

FRANCO: Get used to it. Weekends we get three, four jobs a night out there.

TOMMY: Call it the Indian Burial Ground. Teenagers from Jersey come in to town go to the clubs get drunk and high and then drive home at seven thousand miles an hour trying to make it over the bridge before curfew.

MIKE THE PROBIE: Can't they do something about it? Put some cops out there?

FRANCO: They're kids. They're gonna do what they're gonna do.

TOMMY: Plus it keeps the population a Jersey in check. Think we're all for that.

45

A SAVIOR COMPLEX

LOU: It sounds like your guy's got a savior complex.

MIKE THE PROBIE: What's that?

LOU: You save his life — he feels indebted to you. Happens to all of us. One time I saved this old broad, she had to thank me. Get this — she puts me in her will.

MIKE THE PROBIE: Wow. What happened?

LOU: Nothing. I'm waiting for her to die.

FAKE LEGS

LOU: Paper said it could get to a hundred and five by noon. Perfect day to carry forty-five pounds of gear up and down ten flights of stairs.

SEAN: You know what we need? Shorts. Bunker shorts.

LOU: There's that little problem of your legs burning off.

SEAN: Better than sweating my balls off.

FRANCO: Your balls are more important than your legs?

SEAN: You can get fake legs.

LOU: He's got a point.

LOU: Once we get the bunker shorts, next thing we need? Jet packs. We fly up to the high floors, grab the screaming fire victims and fly them back down to safety.

SEAN: Yeah, but — the jet packs — you have hot exhaust coming out of the engines. That sort of gets in the way of the shorts idea.

LOU: Progress — she's a whore. Back to the drawing board.

MAKING A DIFFERENCE

RED: Listen to me kid — I was a
fireman for fifty goddam years
— a REAL fireman. Before scott
packs and oxygen masks and all
this other pussy goddam breathing
apparatus bullshit. We went into
fires with a cigarette in one
hand and a halligan in the other.
No matter what you think right
now and believe me, every fireman
at some point in his career gets
the jangle — that little bit of
nervous wreck that hits you right
in the ballsack — it's normal,
if you didn't get it THEN you
should start to worry — but you
are making a difference every
goddam day.

LOU: Not today I didn't.

RED: Okay — maybe not every day.
But most days. You toss on them
boots and that gear, you jump on
that rig tomorrow — maybe that's
the day.

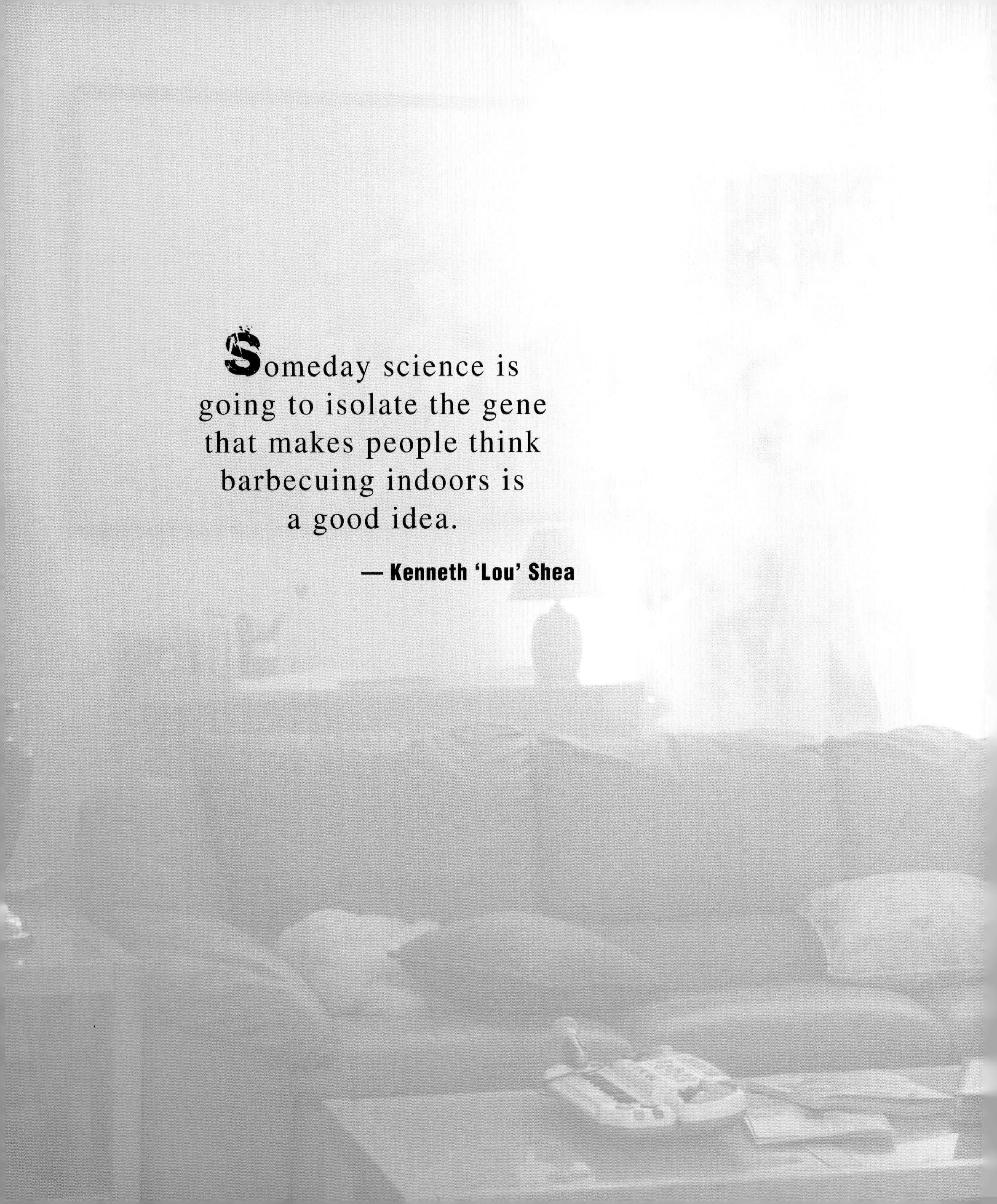

Someday science is
going to isolate the gene
that makes people think
barbecuing indoors is
a good idea.

— **Kenneth 'Lou' Shea**

ALL IN A DAY'S WORK

CARRYING THE BIG GUY

The big black guy, JOHN, sits on the curb getting oxygen. Tommy, Lou and Franco stand with Jerry a few feet away. The guys look like they've been through a struggle.

JERRY: Look at the size of him. No wonder it took you so long getting him out.

LOU: We talked about chopping him up and bringing him down in pieces, but that would've meant an extra trip to get the saw.

AN OXYGEN THING

The guys exit what was a small fire.

MIKE THE PROBIE: Who leaves a space heater on in the middle of the goddam summer?

LOU: Got to be a broad.

TOMMY: Ninety goddam seven outside and they still feel a goddam breeze.

LOU: I think it's an oxygen thing. They talk so much in the course of a day — shoe sales, how screwed up their mothers are, can you believe that shop in Paris wouldn't let Oprah in? Blah blah blah — they got no air left in their bodies. It creates a vacuum — next thing you know? It's Christmas in the middle of July.

SECURITY CAMERAS

JERRY: A couple of young lovebirds decided it might be fun to get it on somewhere between the nineteenth and twentieth floors. They lost track of time —

LOU: Didn't hear the alarm. The throes of passion and all.

JERRY: Cops pulled them out when we were walking in.

SEAN: But you guys went in like twenty minutes ago. What took you?

LOU: Please — we had to look at the footage from the security camera.

JERRY: Several times.

LOU: Don't worry — I'm getting copies made.

THE PERFECT CREW

Frankie — this crew. We got a good crew here. I been through like — when I started I was with a crew that sucked — wrong size guys — four fat guys, one short fat guy with a limp, me, no sense of humor by the book chief — it was a nightmare. When I met you guys — one by one — Lou obviously being the first — by the time Garrity joined I was like — hey, I got the cocky, good-lookin' guy who can kick ass in a fire and still have fun outside it — that bein' you. Garrity? He was a bonus. Strong as a bull. Me, you, Lou and Garrity — Billy too, man, till he got killed. This is a miracle grouping here.

—Tommy Gavin

NO HITTING

SEAN: You're not going to
    hit me again, are you?

TOMMY: Only if it helps.

THE TROUBLE WITH TOMMY

FRANCO: I don't know whether I can believe you or not Tommy. The old Tommy was a lying, cheating, scheming, skirt-chasing son of a bitch — I looked up to him. You always knew where he stood. This new Tommy — the kind sincere honest one? I don't trust him as far as I can throw him.

MISSING DIGITS

JERRY: Your social security number, Mike.
    I think you're missing a few digits.

MIKE: What did I put down?

JERRY: Six.

MIKE: Six digits?

JERRY: No, just the number six. Give
    it another shot.

WITHOUT SIN

LOU: Let he who is without sin cast
    the first stone.

*No response. Lou walks into the
other room. After a beat:*

SEAN: Wow. I never knew Lou was a
    Pink Floyd fan.

*Franco glares at him and exits,
shaking his head in disbelief.*

MIKE: It was Green Day, asshole.

SEAN: Even more impressive!

THE JOB IS EVERYTHING

This person you're talking to right now — I don't know who this guy is. It's me — yeah, of course — but who I am, I got no clue. I was married — thought my wife and I would be together until I got burned up or she put me in the ground with her nonstop talking about bullshit that normal people wouldn't waste breath on — commercials, things she ate that day, why some colors are more healing than others. Now I got no wife. It's like — my life jumped the tracks, and now I'm running on somebody else's tracks, living somebody else's life. (a beat) You're younger than me Laura. You have options — possibilities. If this firefighting gig doesn't work out, you can get married, bake cakes, open a dress shop. I got no future. All I have is today — which right now feels like a yesterday in the making. My job's all I got. It's all I am. Don't make me change how I do it, Laura. One more change and I think I'm done.

— LT. Kenneth 'Lou' Shea

FIREFIGHTERS' HEALTH CONCERNS

PART 1:
CANCER FRIENDLY

LOU: So — the cancer.

RED: My face, my balls — that's it.

LOU: Face and balls — that's pretty
serious.

RED: Hey — my age? Face and balls are
the two least important parts of
my life. Mouth, ass, legs, hands
— in that order, pal. I got to
eat, I got to shit, I got to walk,
I got to pick stuff up. Otherwise?
I'm pretty much cancer friendly.

PART 2:
DANCER CANCER

LOU: I knew Tommy Gavin, sir. Tommy
Gavin was a friend of mine. And that
guy out there is no Tommy Gavin.

SEAN: He's happy. He's smiling.

JERRY: Maybe he's got a disease or
something.

SEAN: Yeah. Is there a kind of cancer
that makes you — dance?

JERRY: Dancer cancer.

LOU: The Travolta Trot.

PART 3:
LANCE

SEAN: Listen, man. I been thinking
— about your nuts — and you really
shouldn't worry about them. One
way or the other you're going to
be fine. Lance Armstrong lost one
of his eggs and look how well he
turned out.

MIKE: Did he lose it before he landed
on the moon?

SEAN: Lance Armstrong. The guy who
won the Tour de France like
twenty-six times in a row?

Mike nods, not quite with it.

SEAN: (cont'd) Shit, you don't know what the Tour de France is either, do you?

MIKE: I want to say wine tasting.

PART 4:
HOLISTIC

SEAN: Double shift. Fun, huh?

SULLY: Not me. I'm out tonight. I got a doctor's appointment.

SEAN: Your doctor works nights?

SULLY: Yeah — he's great. Holistic.

SEAN: (nodding) Holistic. That means — what — something's wrong with your hole?

THE ASS CAMERA

TOMMY: (reading the bulletin board)
Liza Minnelli, Donald Trump,
Geraldo Rivera — what the hell's
this?

LOU: Billy went in for his first time
ever full physical — cameras up
the ass, the whole nine yards.
Results come back tomorrow. He
says if they find some kind of
inoperable cancer, he's going to
kill everyone on that list.

TOMMY: In this order?

Billy *nods yes to Tommy.*

TOMMY: Liza's first, Bill? Hasn't she
suffered enough?

Billy *very calmly nods no.*

SEAN: (to Billy) That ass camera is
really important, Bill. My Dad
wouldn't let them put one up his
ass and now he's dead.

Billy *just stares at him.*

SEAN: Hey, was it, y'know — kind of
. . . uncomfortable? The camera,
I mean.

BILLY: Well, it wasn't really the
camera I minded. It was the crew.

CHLAMYDIA

LOU: Some teacher raped three of her
students.

TOMMY: They say anything about
Chlamydia?

MIKE: You mean the band?

SEAN: It's not a band, asshole,
it's a country.

THE JOB IS ADDICTING

LIFE'S A GAMBLE

INT. McSWEENEY'S PUB — NIGHT
The Chief stands at the bar with several other patrons watching the Browns get obliterated.

JERRY: Jesus Christ — they're playing like they know my bookie. I'm losing on everything — the over, first downs interceptions, sacks. They're killing me.

BAR PATRON: You bet all that stuff? That's some serious gambling.

JERRY: Hey pal — I'm a New York City fireman. My whole life's a goddam gamble.

CIGARETTES

FRANCO: Thought you quit cigarettes.

TOMMY: Right now this ain't a cigarette — it's a flotation device.

NOT DRINKING, TOASTING

DAD: I'm 82. I'm retired. I got my FDNY pension and a new and much younger wife who's not only rich but also likes to bang my brains out at least three times a week. I ain't drinking, kid. I'm in a perpetual toast.

HOW LOW CAN YOU GO?

JIMMY: I honestly didn't think you could go any lower. You're practically at the Earth's core with this shit.

TOMMY: Next stop China.

JOHNNY: Rock bottom doesn't

I'M AN ALCOHOLIC

TOMMY: My name is — Bob. And I'm an alcoholic.

CROWD: Hello Bob!

TOMMY: I — uh — I, um — wanted to say — Look, my Mom was a controlling goddam bitch, too. Now she's dead. My Dad is eighty-something and STILL drinks more than I used to do. Every time I tied up the bathroom growing up he'd remind me that my nose was bigger than my cock and my stepmom is from KOREA, fa crissakes, and based on the only time I met her I'm pretty goddam sure she's a raging alcoholic, too. But the bottom line? I didn't start drinking because my Dad called me a pussy or my Mom said I'd never amount to anything. I drank because — I love to drink. I love whiskey. I love beer. But I could learn to love any form of alcohol you got because I love to drink and I'd still be drinking if it weren't for the fact that I'd lose my job and probably my kids too. So I got to lay off the sauce.

Silence. Almost everyone is offended.

TOMMY: (CONT'D) It ain't you guys who're keeping me from drinking. It's the law. It ain't God who made me stop. It's my soon to be ex-wife. Thanks.

ANOTHER LAP

TOMMY: It's official. My life's gone down the shitter.

LOU: Don't look now. Time for another lap around the bowl.

ONE DAY AT A TIME. . .

MICKEY: Goddammit — what are we doing here Tom? Look, it ain't about how many meetings you go to — it's about the message.

TOMMY: Hey — I know the message Mick. . . Don't drink.

exist for you, does it?

MICKEY: And?

TOMMY: And, um — I — I ain't drinking.

MICKEY: For now! For now Tommy! Because you got the pressure of losing your spot in an active house full of your old friends; because you want to get your kids back and you know Janet's going to bring your drinking up in court — but what about after? Hah? What about next year and the year after and the year after that? Hah? When you run out of reasons to come? When you run out of fake names? Hah? What happens then?

TOMMY: One day at a time, brother. One day at a time.

ACCESSIBLE BOOZE & REPRESSED HOSTILITY

MICKEY: This is where it happens. People in the program who slip up — this is the kind of thing that does it. You can lose a kid — go through serious trauma and stay straight as a goddam arrow and then boom — some innocent little family event. A birthday, a holiday. It's the perfect combination of accessible booze and repressed hostility.

TOMMY: How do you get around it?

MICKEY: I smoke weed.

REUNION

MICKEY: Don't beat yourself up. It happens to a lot of people in the program. You're doing great — you're staying on the straight and narrow — making vast improvement — vast meaning you're only thinking about drinking twenty-three out of every twenty-four hours. Then a bottle finds its way into your hands like an old friend you thought was dead but find out's alive. It all makes for a pretty goddamn glorious reunion.

JUST DON'T DO IT!

TOMMY: Mick, it's me. You up?

MICKEY: I am now. A little early, isn't it?

TOMMY: You're my sponsor. You're
supposed to be available to me
24/7.

MICKEY: I'm honored. What do you
want?

TOMMY: Feel like drinking.

MICKEY: Don't do it.

TOMMY: But I really feel like having
a drink.

MICKEY: Don't do it.

TOMMY: That's all you got. You're
like a bad Nike ad.

PILLS

LOU: Pills. They got pills for everything now. Quit smoking, pay attention, stop worrying, blah blah blah. I'd bet my left ball Janet's on one a these brand new — I hate my husband — I hate my life — my vagina hurts — please make it all go away things.

TOMMY: They got those now?

LOU: Oh yeah. You take two a day, next thing you know your asshole husband is not only funny but you just might want to bang his cheating, deceitful, stupid, little brains out. No offense, Tom.

TOMMY: None taken.

GOOFBALLS

LOU: All of a sudden you're Walt Goddam Whitman over here? There's no way the Tommy Gavin I know writes that poem. There's no way the Tommy Gavin I know writes that poem to seduce his own piece of ass, never mind a buddy's. This, that fall you took, the dancing, the smiling, the goddam cleaning jag — what the hell are you on?

TOMMY: Goofballs. Didn't I tell you?

LOU: No.

TOMMY: Oh. I thought I did. I been swiping Janet's pills. It's great. She loves me, I love her — hey. I love you!

He gives Lou a big smooch on the cheek.

LOU: Tom? Next time you plan on kissing me like that?

TOMMY: Yeah.

LOU: Dinner and a movie first.

TOMMY: Shit, Lou, if this episode, I'd be sweating

72

PLANNING AHEAD

MIKE: Tommy, why do you keep these pills around if you weren't taking 'em anymore?

TOMMY: Duh. Because I'm a junkie.

MIKE: Yeah but — you quit everything.

TOMMY: What if I had a relapse? It was a safety net. So I wouldn't have to go searching for stuff. I was — planning ahead.

was a Columbo
ny balls off.

LOU: For the bender AA is supposed to keep you away from. Nice cult you joined.

IT'S A STEP

INT. FIREHOUSE — LOCKER ROOM
Sean is putting on his shirt. BOOM! a vicious right hook knocks him to the ground. Franco stands over him.

FRANCO: Are you retarded? Scratch that — I KNEW you were retarded, I just didn't think you were THAT retarded.

SEAN: I was going to all those NA meetings and I just got caught up in the whole making amends thingie.

FRANCO: It's not a thingie, it's a step! A step! And you make amends for all your own PERSONAL bullshit! Not mine! Telling Laura I was banging the nurse was one thing, telling the whole crew I was banging Laura — that's like a whole new level of retardation! It's like — the Special Olympics of Substance Abuse.

SEAN: Well — I WAS drunk.

FRANCO: I rest my case!

THIS IS WHERE I LANDED

This is actually a piece of my ass they grafted onto my arm after I punched my way thru a window to pull someone's grandmother out of a raging inferno up in Harlem about fifteen years ago. Shared my mask with her as I brought her back down in the bucket and then — her heart gave out on the way to the hospital.

(He stands back a little and undoes his pants enough to show the top of his right leg: an ugly, ragged scar runs from his hip down his thigh.)

This is where I landed when I was carrying out this drunken asshole who started a fire by smoking in bed and then passed out. Had him on a set a stairs and we both fell through — landed on a set a metal spikes underneath. He lived. Four kids and their mom died. I knew sixty guys who died on 9/11 and I guarantee more people in this bar know the names of the last five finalists on this year's American Idol than they do one name — one goddam name — of the 343 firemen who gave their lives that day. . . I got no wallet or cash 'cause someone stole my truck this morning — I got a firefighter buddy in the burn unit they just cut off both his legs — my wife is pregnant but we don't know who's baby it is 'cause she's having sex with me AND my brother. My uncle's in jail for killing the drunk driver who ran over my only son last summer and I just saw said dead son riding on a crosstown bus right outside this goddam bar.

— **Tommy Gavin**

FEEDING THE FIREMEN

PART 1:
PIE

SEAN: How am I an idiot?

LOU: Let me count the ways.

SEAN: Ask anybody. Blueberry pie
counts as fruit.

TOMMY: It's pie, asshole. Pie isn't a
fruit. Pie doesn't grow on bushes
or trees. You don't go out into
the fields to harvest pie.

LOU: But what a beautiful world if
you could.

PART 2:
GREEN TEA

LOU: Tom, you forgot my green tea.

TOMMY: The day you see me order green
tea in a coffee shop is the day I
put a gun in my mouth.

PART 3:
SANDWICHES

The rig barrels along. The guys are enjoying sandwiches.

MIKE: I know it's out of the way, but any time you guys want to cross town for one of these grinders — I'm in.

TOMMY: Grinders?

SEAN: It's a hero, dipshit.

FRANCO: Where the hell are these terms coming from?

TOMMY: Ted Williams is a hero. John Kennedy — hero. This is meat and bread. It's a goddamn sandwich. Assholes.

PART 4:
BEEFSTACHIO

Tommy enters the bedroom where all three of his children are sleeping. Uncle Teddy sits in a nearby chair — eating ice cream and steak.

TOMMY: Ice cream and steak?

UNCLE TEDDY: My latest thing. Beefstachio. I called the people at Ben 'N Jerry's — gave 'em the recipe? They said no. Some people got no vision.

PART 5:
CHINK FOOD AND BIRTHDAY CAKE

DAD: Are you kidding? There's going to be Chink food and birthday cake. You can't have a disaster with that combination. If they served Chink food and birthday cake at Normandy? World War II? Over!

TOMMY: I hate pulp — orang band Pulp, Pulp Fiction

juice pulp, British
Quentin Goddam Tarantino.

SENSITIVITY TRAINING

DON: Okay, we have a hand raised. You think you're prejudiced?

TOMMY: Yup.

DON: Against?

TOMMY: Chevy Neons that cost twelve grand to buy but have eight thousand dollar paint jobs on them and nine spicks packed inside smoking weed.

DON: See now, the term spick —

FRANCO: It's okay — I'm a spick —

DON: Oh. Well, I don't think that —

TOMMY: Crazy chink broads who don't know how to drive in the first place and now they got cell phones pressed against their ears. Crazy chinks on bikes going 40 mph, ten pounds of Chinese food strapped to the handlebars, no helmets —

DON: Okay now, just — chink is what I like to call a — problem word.

SEAN: Hey — if I were a chink I'd prefer chink over gook.

DON: Okay — listen to me. Chinese people would not like chink OR gook. Or panface. Or zipperhead.

FRANCO: See? That's another thing. Puerto Ricans — we get shafted even when it comes to racism. Chinks got what — four ethnic slurs? We got one — spick. That's it. The Irish got mick, paddy, donkey. The Italians got dago, guinea and wop.

SEAN: Spaghetti bender.

FRANCO: Spaghetti bender went out of style during Sinatra's first marriage.

MIKE THE PROBIE: Greaseball.

FRANCO: Okay greaseball — that's

LOU: Like Rain Man retarded

four. Again. And black guys
— spearchucker, junglebunny,
raisinhead, porchmonkey —

LOU: Spook.

TOMMY: Shine.

SEAN: Tarbaby.

FRANCO: It's endless. And totally
unfair.

INNER RACIST

TOMMY: Cops are on the case. What's
the goddam city coming to? Twelve
minutes I owned the goddam car.

LOU: Need I remind you how far uptown
our house is located?

FRANCO: Glad to see you haven't lost
touch with your inner racist, Lou.

WHY PUERTO RICANS DON'T PLAY HOCKEY

FRANCO: Now you know why Puerto
Ricans don't play hockey.

SEAN: Why's that?

FRANCO: We'd all be carrying knives.
It'd be a bloodbath out there.

MAGGIE: Not to mention all the
hubcaps would be stolen off
the zamboni.

or Paris Hilton retarded?

CAN A WOMAN BE A FIREFIGHTER?

DR. GOLDBERG: Are you threatened by women? You don't seem to think that a woman can be a firefighter.

TOMMY: This ain't about being a man or a woman. It's about doing the job. Either you can do it or you can't. Life or death. I want to come back safe 'n sound and see my kids in the morning. You got a woman better than the guys I got on my crew already? Bring her on. You got a martian or a cyborg or a Chinaman? Bring them on, too.

COMPUTERIZED BROAD

LOU: Automated system. And they had to make it a woman's voice. Politically correct bullshit.

LOU: That voice is the closest I'll ever get to working with a broad.

JERRY: A computerized broad is running my goddam life right now.

WE'RE GETTING A DAME

JERRY: Let me just say this, huh? When we lost Bill, headquarters said they were gonna send us a transfer to take his place. Well, that's happening — but — Those goddamn bastards. We're getting a dame.

FRANCO: Chief, is there any way around this?

JERRY: I kicked and screamed — so did Perrolli, believe it or not — but it's a done deal. We're getting a broad within the next couple of days.

LOU: This is not going to work! Having a woman in the house — it's disruptive, it's destructive. The dynamic we've got going here —

JERRY: Calm down.

LOU: Don't tell me to calm down! Forget about what happens in the house. These goddamn chicks — they can't even pass the physical. The bean counters downtown lower the standards so they can meet their bitch quota.

FRANCO: Like they give a shit. We're the ones who'll have to go into a big fire with one of these whores. She'll break a nail, go to pieces, and we're the ones who'll wind up dead. . . .

LOU: They want to send us a dame? I'll tell you what we're gonna do, boys. We're going to freeze her ass out. Totally. From the first second she walks in the door. Ice. She won't last two days.

ICE

LAURA: Excuse me, guys. Is Chief Reilly here?

JERRY: Can I help you?

LAURA: I'm Laura Miles. I've been transferred to your house.

Lou raises a finger to the crew.

LOU: Ice.

He turns and walks out. All of the other guys follow suit.

LAURA: Oh, okay. Nice. Thanks. Very adult. Appreciate it.

FORMAL WEAR

LAURA: (back still turned) I know you guys are talking about my tits and my ass.

They all freeze. Long beat as she keeps working.

LAURA: (cont'd) Just in case you are wondering — I'm a 34 C cup, my left tit is a little bit bigger than my right, I have slightly larger than normal size nipples which stand up like top hats at the slightest hint of arousal, my ass is as tight as a snare drum but still soft to the touch, and I don't believe in a full Brazilian bikini wax so my pussy is that of a normal happy 30 year old woman — and matches the hair on my head.

She drops a magnificent looking sandwich in front of Tommy.

LAURA: (cont'd) Any other questions?

SEAN: Um (off the sandwich) — can I get one of those?

LAURA: Nope.

TOMMY: Did she say top hats?

FRANCO: Yes she did.

LOU: I've always been a big fan a formal wear.

LOVELUMP

Here comes Laura — looking great. She stops and clicks a quick picture of the outside of the house with a disposable camera.

JERRY: You're ten minutes late, sweetheart.

LAURA: Sorry, darling.

JERRY: Excuse me?

LAURA: You call me names, from now on you're getting them right back.

JERRY: Don't push it, dolly.

LAURA: Okay, lovelump.

Laura exits into the house.

JERRY: (to Lou) Lovelump?

LOU: I've used it.

TWAT

INT. FIREHOUSE - KITCHEN
Mike's trying to ease the tensions:

MIKE: I thought the word women hated
    was the 'c' word.

SEAN: Yeah. I thought they invented
    twat so no one would ever have to
    say — the other one — ever again.

LAURA: I think men invented both and never
    checked with women about either.

Franco enters, feeling more relaxed.

TOMMY: What would you prefer? A
    brand new word? A combination
    of the two?

SEAN: (quick thinking) Cwat? *Everyone
    gives him a look.*

TOMMY: Twunt.

Franco laughs. Laura glares at him.

He recovers with:

FRANCO: C'mon — that's funny.

MIKE: Twunt. Like it.

TOMMY: (side of the mouth) You're not
    helping my case here kid.

SEAN: I'm sticking with cwat.

FRANCO: Nobody likes it, Sean.

SEAN: Oh yeah? Let's ask Laura. She's
    the only one who matters in this
    particular case. She's the person
    in this room who is most affected
    by either one of the words. Laura?
    What's your opinion?

LAURA: I actually find cwat to be
    even more offensive than twat
    — monkeyboy.

INT. FIREHOUSE - KITCHEN - SAME
The discussion continues.

FRANCO: Laura, look — this shit
    doesn't mean anything around here.
    I call Tommy a Mick, he calls me
    a Spic, Sean calls Mike a stupid
    Guinea —

MIKE: Hey!

FRANCO: I know I know, you're not
    stupid — we all use every ethnic and
    personal slur in the book against
    each other. You name it, we say it.

TOMMY: Cockbreath.

FRANCO: Shithead.

SEAN: Asswipe.

MIKE: Numbnuts.

TOMMY: Ballface.

FRANCO: Shit-for-brains.

SEAN: Dipshit.

MIKE: Pussy.

TOMMY: Prick.

FRANCO: Dick.

SEAN: Scumbag.

TOMMY: Dickface.

FRANCO: Ape-ass.

MIKE: Apeface.

TOMMY: Pencildick.

MIKE: Tightass.

FRANCO: Needledick.

TOMMY: Nimrod.

FRANCO: And that's not even getting
    into any of the gay stuff.

LAURA: Well — that's debatable.

COURAGE AND THE CREW

The day after 9/11, when it began to dawn on us who had and who hadn't come out of those towers — guys like me and Lou and even Franco became senior members of the department overnight. Then even more guys my age got waylaid because after we were done digging through the dirt and the rubble trying to find first the bodies and then the belt buckles and then just maybe one goddam tooth from each of our fallen brothers — some of us couldn't breathe out all the crap we'd been breathing in.

(Tommy lost in thought. This next part hurts more than you think it should:)

Some of the guys — some of them just — couldn't take it anymore. So — a crew like this? A good team with the right balance between age and experience and different abilities? This ain't something you come across every day. I love this job — and I trust all of you. *(looks at Laura)* For the most part. I don't go into burning buildings with the Bible in my back pocket or with God by my side. I go in with you. All of you. And when we come back out and get back here — part of the job is busting balls and owning up. What you did wrong. What you won't do wrong again. Priorities.

You can't legislate courage. No judge on earth can order you to give enough of a shit about other people to run into eight floors full of flame. It takes guts. And a good crew you trust with your own life.

(to Laura) You let Lou down. He called you a twat. Get over it. The real issue is — next time? In a fire? Will you be where you're supposed to be? Twat, cwat, bitch or twunt? The real issue? Do your job the right way and people call you names you like to be called.

— **Tommy Gavin**

BECAUSE I'M A GIRL

LAURA: This firefighting thing — this wasn't some lark, you know. I saw a news story about a female firefighter when I was seven years old, and — my mind was made up. I wanted to be just like her. I told my father — he laughed in my face. "You? You can't do that job, sweetheart. You're a girl!" He used to dine out on that story — lots of laughs. Every boyfriend I ever had — "You can't do that! You're a girl!"

Every guy I met at the academy. "You don't belong here, bitch. You're a girl." But I stuck with it and broke my back and toughened my hide and cried when nobody was looking — and I became a firefighter, goddamn it. I got assigned to a house, I actually started doing the job — and what was my next course of action? Falling in love with a guy on my crew. Because he was hot and sweet and I thought he needed me on some level — and because I'm a girl. I came all this way and that's what I found out. My father was right — I'm just a girl. And I've got nobody to blame but myself.

SAVAGE PRICKS

LAURA: That goddamn firehouse. The lying, the cheating, the back stabbing, the stupid gags. Not to mention the latent homosexuality that runs rampant through the halls. I might as well be working in a nut house.

DAWN: What did you expect, huh? Chess tournaments and tea parties? Maybe a book club?

LAURA: I expected to see at least one of these idiots get tired of dragging his knuckles along the floor and move forward — evolve. Do something productive.

DAWN: Well, they do save lives. Some would consider that productive.

LAURA: I'm not talking about the job. They do that as well as anybody. But emotionally? It's like they're trapped in the sixth grade.

DAWN: I hate to be the one to break this to you, sweetie — but you just encapsulated the entire gender. Here's to them — the savage pricks.

WAY TO GO, PART 1

EXT. SIDEWALK — LATER 13
Perolli, Lou and Tommy walk over to a couple of EMTs. One of the EMTs stands next to a body covered in a sheet. The shape of the body is odd — the sheet is tented. A police officer stands at the entrance to a nearby apartment building.

PEROLLI: *(to the EMT)* What we got?

EMT GUY: — Middle Eastern, thirty years of age, give or take — impaled by a tree branch.

PEROLLI: A tree branch? In the middle of Manhattan?

EMT GUY: *(pointing up)* Rooftop garden. Dead branch broke off in the wind — bam.

LOU: Talk about getting wood.

TOMMY: From the look of things, he's still got it.

LOU: Maybe we should go up to the roof, talk to the tree. I mean, it looks like an accident, but you never know.

TOMMY: Maybe there's some shrubs up there saw something. I say we uproot the whole damn garden, bring it in for questioning.

LOU: Just because it's vegetation, it thinks it can get away with this shit.

WAY TO GO, PART 2

Franco pulls a copy of last year's calendar out of his car and opens it to a certain month.

FRANCO: You see this guy? He was gonna be Mr. March this year only he's dead. Guy was insane. Ran with the bulls a couple times. Did that skiing thing where they drop you onto a mountain out of a helicopter. Swam with sharks, did low-altitude parachuting —

SEAN: How did he die?

FRANCO: Fell in the tub.

WAY TO GO, PART 3

LOU: How would you rather go? Burned up, fighting, getting pieces taken off of you like Stack did; like you're Mr. Potato Head. They just pull off your legs and pull off your hands or THIS way; banging your brains out with your cock as hard as rock. I am dead serious Tom. Mr. Potato Head style or cock like a shovel?

FIREFIGHTER BILLY'S FUNERAL

INT. HIBERNIAN HALL

JERRY: We all knew Billy Warren as a firefighter's firefighter. He knew each and every building in his district like the back of his hand. He was dedicated and devout when it came to protecting the public. He was a brave, brave man. Billy left very specific orders if he were to be killed in the line of duty. He didn't want a funeral mass or a burial. He wanted everyone to gather together and celebrate his life. He wanted everyone to remember him with a smile on their faces. And he wanted his ex-wife to speak in his memory. She is here today to do just that.

He nods and an absolutely gorgeous forty-year-old woman — one you would never expect to see at Billy's side — steps up.

SONDRA: *(not crying)* Hello. My name is Sondra Warren. Most of you probably don't know who I am. That's because Billy and I were only married for six weeks about fifteen years ago. Knowing Billy, he probably never mentioned me to you. Because I discovered three weeks into our marriage that Billy was still having an affair with his old girlfriend Mary. Mary?

TOMMY: If there is a God he' shitload of explainin,

(She looks around the hall.) There she is. Stand up Mare.

Mary — even more stunning than Sondra — gives a quick wave. The guys can't believe what they are seeing.

SONDRA: You see — Billy didn't really love me. Or Mary, for that matter. He loved you guys. The fire department. The guys on his crew — I heard these names a lot — Tommy, Jerry, Lou, Franco. Stand up guys.

They do. Very awkward waves.

SONDRA: Nice to connect the names with the faces. A lot of you guys would never admit that you feel closer to the guys at the firehouse than you do to your own wives or kids. We all see you as heroic and brave and — whatever — and we forgive you your sins. As if you were not mere mortals. But that's what you are. When someone sets fire to you — you burn the

same way the people you are trying to save do. And if you choose to get married — if you choose to start a family — I'm sorry, but you owe us something too. A little love. A little attention. A little more than the occasional wham bam thank you ma'am. I'm sorry Billy died. But I'm glad he died in the line of duty because that's the way he would have wanted it. And I'm not going to miss him because I wrote him out of my life the day I found out he was still seeing Mary behind my back. Thank you.

ot a whole
o do.

97

JOHNNY'S FUNERAL

DAD: Here's the deal. No black suits.
No black ties. No black dresses.
The only formal clothes will be
his police brethren in their dress
blues. I want everyone in colors.
Bright colors. Like spring in
bloom. I want to celebrate my kid's
life, not his death — what he did
while he was on this planet — how
he almost always put a smile on my
face every time he walked into a
room I was in. *(a beat)* And Red?

UNCLE RED: Yeah.

DAD: We're gonna need a lot more
whiskey.

MY IMMORTAL WALLET

TOMMY: What — uhh. What would you do
if — I got killed at work today or
dropped dead five seconds from now.

*Janet sighs again. Turns back. Steps
up to him.*

JANET: One Mississippi, two
Mississippi —

TOMMY: Very funny. What would you do?
For money.

JANET: Sell your truck and this house
for starters.

*She said it so quickly that Tommy is
thrown.*

JANET: *(cont'd)* You have an unhealthy
obsession with leaving this life
Tommy.

TOMMY: No I —

JANET: Yes you do. You have some kind
of death wish going on?

TOMMY: I ain't afraid to die, if
that's what you're asking. 'Cause
wherever it is we're going, I know
I'm going to see Jimmy and Billy
and —

JANET: Yeah, yeah, yeah. Keep it up
and you'll get there pretty goddam
fast. Because just like Billy's ex
said at his service — you are not
immortal.

TOMMY: No. But apparently my wallet
is.

THE AFTERLIFE IN MIKE'S PANTS

INT. FIREHOUSE — KITCHEN — THE NEXT DAY
*Franco, Mike, Sean, Lou and Tommy are
eating and bullshitting around the
table.*

FRANCO: *(to Mike)* So how long you
    planning on sleeping here?

MIKE THE PROBIE: Until I find a new
    place. If you guys hear about a
    real cheap studio apartment, let
    me know, okay?

LOU: Trouble in paradise, junior?

SEAN: He got caught banging his
    girlfriend's daughter.

LOU: I don't believe this kid. People
    are asking him to do three-ways,
    he's doing the mother-daughter
    combo platter — I never thought
    I'd say this, but when I die, I'd
    like to come back as your penis.

NEVER MISSED A DAY OF WORK

Tommy lying on the couch with a cold compress on his face. His Dad enters.

DAD: So. You didn't go to work today. (*no answer*) I never missed a day a work in my life. They had to chase me out of the goddam firehouse after every goddam tour. I loved it.

TOMMY: And — you hated mom.

DAD: Well — that too. But I could drink my ass off without crying. Pussy.

Tommy's cell rings. He answers it.

TOMMY: Yeah. This is he. Great. Really. Perfect. Thanks.

DAD: Who was that — Barry Manilow?

TOMMY: They found my truck. In one piece. Guy got drunk and fell asleep behind the wheel, parked over on Riverside.

DAD: Jesus Christ. Nobody knows how to drink and drive anymore.

DYING BREED

TOMMY: Tell you, man — the FDNY? Ain't the way it used to be. Full of bean counters and brown-nosers now. Straight arrows. Guys like me? We're a dying breed.

EDDIE: Yeah. All that drinking and drugging — the mistresses. The lying, the cheating. What's the world coming to?

REAL FAMILY

TOMMY: (*to Lou*) What — you — you don't think I've thought about getting out before? It doesn't work. Guys like us are not meant for the normal world. This house is our home. Especially for you and me right now — this — this is our family. Only real family we got left.

PERROLLI: Probie's transferring.

LOU: Call Dr. Phil. Maybe he can help.

EPIPHANY

LOU: I had an epiphany, Tom.

TOMMY: An epiphany. What's that, something you got at Quizno's?... Know who else had an epiphany.

LOU: Who?

TOMMY: Hitler. Next thing you know? No more bagels and cream cheese in downtown Berlin.

WHY FLORIDA?

TOMMY: Bad idea. Absolutely. First off — Florida. Old people, tornadoes, Jeb Bush — bugs — gigantic bugs the size of your bike there. Then this boat — nightmare. You're out there with tourists, kids — everybody's puking. You pull in your line, you're catching Great Whites, alligators — Cubans trying to swim to freedom. And then there's the whole Bermuda Triangle issue, which is a real situation if we can believe the Discovery Channel. Florida's a shitty idea, Lou. Forget about it.

LOU: I guess you don't remember me asking for a little support.

STUCK

ou get in a groove, get the right group of guys together, the energy the laughs the sense of timing blah blah blah — things click. There's nothing like it. These guys — I'd walk into the fiery gates of hell with these guys and know for a goddam fact we were coming back out fifteen minutes later without so much as a mark on any one of us. I can't start over. They're all kids now — most of the vets got out after 9/11. I'll either kill myself trying to train them or they'll get me killed on a call. I'm stuck.

— **Tommy Gavin**

LADDER 62

CHAPTER 2
SEX

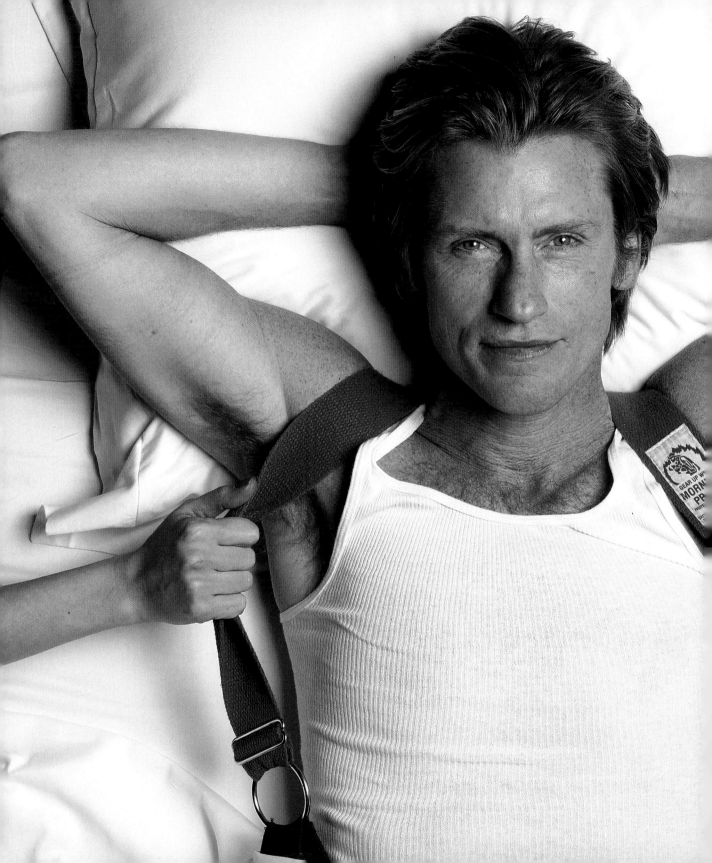

THE RULES AMONG FIREFIGHTERS

RULE 1 You don't bang a guy's girlfriend, ex-girlfriend, ex-wife, wife or sister without his permission — meaning his crystal clear permission.

RULE 2 You can run into a guy's ex-girlfriend and feel her up. Yes.

RULE 3 You can run into a guy's ex-wife at a bar and get a little bit of titty action. You can grab a guy's sister's ass in a bar that the guy happens to be in and it's okay. And it's all explained under the giant umbrella of the huge "I was drunk" rule. Like Visa and Master Card: accepted the world over.

RULE 4 We have sex with women who ain't our wives — we make every detail available to the other guys. Not only for the sheer entertainment value, but also for the possible educational and historical value. Not to mention keeping ourselves up-to-date on what the other side might be thinking and/or doing.

RULE 5 You start banging a brother-sister team, you're required to share that. By law. Geneva convention.

CHANNELING TOMMY

TOMMY: C'mon, Lou. Nobody forgets to file divorce papers. Sounds to me like this twist gets off on the whole infidelity thing. Where'd you two leave it?

LOU: Well, I was totally off guard. She asked if I was seeing anybody.

TOMMY: And?

LOU: I tried to channel you.

TOMMY: Jesus — how many times I got to tell you guys? Don't channel me — pretend you got to take a piss and —

LOU: — call your cell! I know I know!

TOMMY: It's not something I learned!

LOU: It's a gift! I know. (a beat) I tap danced through this lie with the grace of an ox.

TOMMY: Let's hear it.

LOU: I set the bar way too high. Described the imaginary girlfriend as the most amazing woman on the planet. You know, the type I'd never get in a million years.

TOMMY: Yeesh. She buy it?

LOU: Hard to say. She seemed to enjoy watching me squirm. Now she wants to see me out with the imaginary girlfriend. I'm done for.

TOMMY: Not necessarily. Situations like this are why God invented whores.

LOU: I never even thought of whores.

TOMMY: Black Tony from Ladder 68 gets whores on the internet all the time. You surf the web, you click the mouse — voila! Any type of girl you want at your door within 45 minutes.

LOU: It really is a gift.

TOMMY: From God. Or Satan. That's the problem with gifts. No card? No credit.

TALK TO YOUR GODSON

SHEILA: You got to talk to Damien. I found a box of condoms in his room.

TOMMY: He's almost eighteen, there's porn all over the internet — straight, gay, hardcore, soft core, midgets blowing sheep — I think he's probably pretty up to date. Besides, having a box of condoms doesn't necessarily mean he's using them.

SHEILA: You're his godfather.

TOMMY: I won't know what to say.

SHEILA: Tell him what your father told you.

TOMMY: 'Don't wipe your dick on the drapes'?

SHEILA: That's disgusting.

TOMMY: That's what he told me. Along with 'eating ain't cheating' and 'blow jobs don't count'.

SHEILA: Is that true?

TOMMY: Not since Clinton got busted.

THE HISTORY OF HARD-ONS

ANGIE: Okay. This is officially the longest lasting hard-on in the history of hard-ons.

TOMMY: Actually — I had one when I was thirteen that lasted pretty much all the way through freshman year.

FIFTEEN MINUTES

ANGIE: Damn right it's you. I've never had a problem getting a guy off. Every guy I've ever been with — they couldn't hold off longer than two minutes. Johnny, Red Scott, Timmy Scavone, Father Doug from St. Francis, Joe Torre's nephew, Billy Lynch —

TOMMY: Whoa, whoa. Father Doug?

ANGIE: Yeah. Actually, that one took about fifteen minutes — then again it was Easter. And it was over the phone.

TOMMY GAVIN'S DATING ADVICE

FOR THE TEENAGE BOY BANGING HIS SCIENCE TEACHER

Women are tough, Damien. The only advice I can give you is stick to girls while it's still legal. You got the rest of your life to get kicked around by women.

DO NOT WRITE ABOUT THE ASS

Write about how nice her tits are. Women love to hear how much you love the way they look. Their lips, their eyes but stay away from the ass. All women — young, old, Cindy Crawford on her best goddam day — hate their ass and think it's too fat. I'm with you brother on how great the ass — no matter how big they think it might be — feels to us — it's a dream location chock full of fun but to them? The ass is death. Death, gravity, and hard goddam times. Stick with lips. The lips on her face. Eyes. Eyelashes. Tits.

MAKE SOME SPACE

Look Laura — when it comes to sex, for men? Even when it's love — absence makes the heart grow fonder. These couples you see who live AND work together — Lucy and Desi, JLo and Ben, Ben and Matt, even Siegfried and Roy — they all crash and burn. They end up in ugly divorce or spiteful separation or with an exotic animal biting one or the other's head off. Lovers need space. That's where you got crossed up. Franco probably feels suffocated. Maybe you do too. Just be thankful there's no wild animals working in the firehouse.

WOMEN ARE SO COMPLICATED

It's always so goddamn complicated with women. It's not enough you're banging them, you have to know their names, too.

THE PENIS-BRAIN CONNECTION

Shit! Listen — there's all kinds of weird connections between your penis and your brain. Ever look behind the scenes at your Mom's home entertainment system? It's full of cables and wires and inputs and outputs. Well, your dick and your brain work the same way — you connect the wrong input to the wrong output — well, pretty soon you got a thing for older women stuck in your brain which is wired to your dick and then all of a sudden your entire pleasure center is a mess. Instead of banging hot Mrs. Turbody when she's 38 and your 18, you'll find yourself at 45 years old trying to bang a broad who's almost seventy. Ever seen your grandmother naked?

They're so — bendable.

MAKE THE MOST OF THOSE SCARS

TOMMY: Let me see the scar.

Franco pulls his collar down and shows Tommy his neck.

TOMMY: Not too bad. You got to be getting some serious tail with that.

FRANCO: Tell you the truth — I was embarrassed about it for awhile — thought it made me look scary. Now I wish it was bigger. Some girls don't even see it. I gotta twist around, put my neck in their face. It gets complicated.

TOMMY: What do you tell them?

FRANCO: Depends. Sometimes I say I got it pulling some kids out of a fire at a school. Depends on the chick.

TOMMY: You see this? I used to tell girls I got this in a huge fire saving an old blind lady's cat. Never failed.

FRANCO: Where did you really get it?

TOMMY: Put my arm through a window fooling around with my little brother when I was six. You can see why I went with the old blind lady.

FRANCO: I like that. I think I'm going make the kids in my story blind.

TOMMY: Take it.

FRANCO: Thanks.

PEOPLE FORGET

TOMMY: What I don't believe is you making a move on a chick with sideburns — chick sideburns yes, but sideburns nonetheless.

FRANCO: Hey Tommy — it's slowing down out there, pal. All that pussy I was getting after 9/11 — now nothing. People forget.

TOMMY: Yup. It's a sad commentary.

STUPID

ANGIE: This is incredibly stupid.

TOMMY: You're in luck. Incredibly stupid is one of my best things.

HOTLINE

TOMMY: This is the emergency?

SHEILA: Yes. It was an emotional
    emergency.

TOMMY: Do me a favor — next time
    call The Hormone Hotline.

KARMA

JIMMY: Ironic, ain't it? You jump
    into the sack with my wife and
    now here you are — your own
    brother putting it to your wife.
    Ironic. Definition of the word.

TOMMY: No.

JIMMY: No. Okay. What is it then?
    Enlighten me.

TOMMY: Karma.

JIMMY: You're right. It is karma. I
    stand corrected.

TOMMY: Uh-huh. You know the thing
    about karma — it just keeps going
    around and around and around...

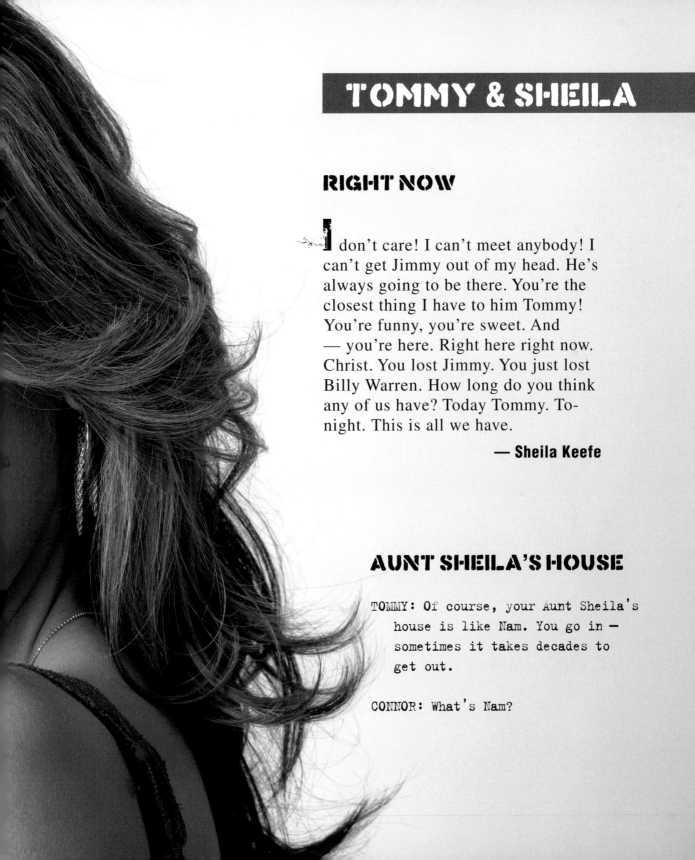

TOMMY & SHEILA

RIGHT NOW

I don't care! I can't meet anybody! I can't get Jimmy out of my head. He's always going to be there. You're the closest thing I have to him Tommy! You're funny, you're sweet. And — you're here. Right here right now. Christ. You lost Jimmy. You just lost Billy Warren. How long do you think any of us have? Today Tommy. To-night. This is all we have.

— **Sheila Keefe**

AUNT SHEILA'S HOUSE

```
TOMMY: Of course, your Aunt Sheila's
    house is like Nam. You go in —
    sometimes it takes decades to
    get out.

CONNOR: What's Nam?
```

THE LIST GOES ON

1 She's the kind of girl I call a firecracker. She's got one good bang in her — that's about it.

2 I've dated bartenders, never works out. They're appealing when they're serving you drinks and there's three feet of pine between you, but once the buffer's gone there's no getting away from them.

3 I'm banging this chick but I've never seen her out with people. If she eats the way she gets it on — hell, nobody needs to see that.

4 The difference between older and younger chicks? The old ones know what they're doing, but they've been through it so many times, it's mechanical. The young ones aren't as good, but they still have the fellatio enthusiasm.

5 There's no greater way to measure how much you love someone than by how far you'll go to hurt them.

Love's a pain in the balls.

SEX AND THE CHIEF

EARTHA KITT?

JERRY: Yeah. S'like — banging Mary Tyler Moore? I got that covered. But Eartha Kitt? That's a different story.

TOMMY: Jesus Jerry — I'd need four Viagras, a blindfold and a seven inch strap-on to do either one.

LIPS

JERRY: Says here that Brad Pitt and Angelina Jolie got 4 million bucks for the exclusive rights to the first pictures of their baby.

SEAN: 4 million bucks. Holy shit.

LOU: For 4 million bucks I'd give you the pictures AND the goddam kid.

FRANCO: I'd give you the pics, the kid AND Angelina. I don't like those lips.

LOU: Me neither. Too big. Makes your cock look smaller.

THINGS TO DO IN NYC

JERRY: It's an underground sex club.

FRANCO: No shit.

JERRY: New York City — greatest city in the world. Statue of Liberty, Empire State Building, Central Park. So many things to see and do — but no — they'd rather be in some dingy basement hanging from the ceiling in a sling with a rubber ball in their mouth and a rope around their nuts.

FRANCO: On the other hand, Chief — how many times can you visit the Statue of Liberty?

JERRY: True.

THE WORLD ACCORDING TO LOU

MY DREAMS

LOU: Kid — my dreams are all full up with Candice Bergen and chocolate condoms. Not ta mention Elizabeth Taylor in a wheelchair — naked.

JERRY: I've had that same dream.

TOMMY: Me too. Except it was Elizabeth Hurley. And the wheelchair was optional.

LIFE SUPPORT

LOU: Remember this broad? The chick that was on life support for fifteen years. Her husband had them pull the plug.

MIKE THE PROBIE: Yeah, but her parents wanted to keep her alive.

TOMMY: It's so sad.

FRANCO: She was bulimic or anorexic.

LOU: She was both. That's how she got into the coma — her body was weak and she had a massive heart attack. They finally let her go.

TOMMY: But what if she suddenly woke up one morning?

LOU: You know what she'd say if she SUDDENLY woke up one morning?

FRANCO: What?

LOU: Does my ass look fat in this bed?

FORBIDDEN FRUIT

JERRY: Divorce is a bitch. At least you got your girlfriend.

LOU: Yeah, but she's only into un-available men. Now that the wife is gone —

JERRY: Your fruit is no longer forbidden.

LOU: I told her, "I'm easy. Flat bacon. Hot coffee. An afternoon blowjob three or four times a week." She didn't bite.

JERRY: So, it's over.

LOU: Unless I remarry or get involved with someone else — then we're back on.

THIS INVOLVED PRAYER

LOU: This is wrong. This is so
    wrong. Move a little to the
    left. That's it! Honey —
    listen, I'm into edgy, kind
    of out there, public sex as
    much as the next guy — but in
    a choir loft during mass? I
    mean, that's probably — I dunno
    — the third ring of hell?

THERESA: I'm guessing first ring.
    (*moaning*) Oh, God. Oh, God.

LOU: Yeah, keep that up — if we get
    caught, I can honestly say there
    was prayer involved.

If it wasn't for my wife,
my high blood pressure and
my decreased sex drive, I'd
be on that like white on rice.

— Kenneth "Lou" Shea

GOOD TO GO

PAULA: Do you smoke?

MIKE THE PROBIE: No.

PAULA: Are you a Republican?

MIKE THE PROBIE: No.

PAULA: Then we're good to go.

She kisses him violently.

FISH IN A BARREL

MIKE: Try and straighten up. Two hot chicks in a room full of gay guys? This'll be like catching fish in a barrel.

SEAN: Shooting fish.

MIKE: What?

SEAN: Shooting fish in a barrel is the expression, you dumb shit.

MIKE: If they're in the barrel, why would you shoot them? Why wouldn't you just reach in with your hands —

SEAN: Okay, okay — let's just hit on the girls. Come on.

WASTED ON THE YOUNG

LOU: So what did you do?

MIKE THE PROBIE: I excused myself, went into the bath-room and stayed there for an hour and a half. They finally went home.

LOU: Wait a minute. You actually passed up a three-way? Was the girl hot?

MIKE THE PROBIE: Way hot.

LOU: Are you insane?

MIKE THE PROBIE: Lou, I would've had to have sex in front of another guy.

LOU: So block him out.

MIKE THE PROBIE: What if I got hit with — friendly fire?

LOU: Make sure you finish first and get the hell out of the way. Jesus! It's true what they say — three-ways, like youth, are wasted on the young.

BLOW JOB ETIQUETTE

CHRIS: So all those times I was going down on you — you weren't comfortable? You sure seemed comfortable to me, Mike. I mean, if you didn't like it, why didn't you speak the hell up?

MIKE: You know how it is — when somebody's going down on you, you don't want to be rude.

TWO DEAD CHICKS

SEAN: This is serious. I got two dead chicks on my conscience — Nez and Kate — and I'm starting to think it's got something to do with my mojo, you know? Like, my dick's some kind of weapon of mass destruction.

LOU: First of all, your cock is not a weapon of mass destruction. If it were I'd be in complete awe of you — which I'm not. The real issue is there is something wrong with your dating pool. It should be drained and filled in, with blacktop over it.

SMOKING AND SEX

SEAN: I smoked because of sex with my girlfriend.

FRANCO: Oh, the old cigarette after sex.

SEAN: Actually, it was during. She was on top — smoking — and I just couldn't concentrate — couldn't get the job done watching her — inhale. So I lit up — bing, bang, boom — the saints went marching in.

SHE DOES THIS THING

LOU: How long you been seeing her?

SEAN: Thirty-three days. (*catching himself*) Thirty-three and a half, really, because the first day was a morning thing where we just — ran into each other but — I count it.

JERRY: So you're really, really in love here.

SEAN: She's got the greatest set of tits I've ever seen.

TOMMY: Unbelievable.

MAGGIE: You wouldn't want a
You wouldn't be abl

SEAN: And she does this thing
with her toes where she takes
my cock 'n —

LOU: Another healthy relationship
for 62 Truck.

SEAN: It's like she knows — magic.

TOMMY: Somebody call Dr. Phil.

WHOSE PORN IS IT?

MAGGIE: You're throwing the porn out?

SEAN: You know, a lot of women —
wives — would be thrilled to see
their guy throwing out the porn.
That's a major, huge step in a
marriage. It shows commitment and
maturity and I think you should
take it as a very positive thing.

MAGGIE: Yeah, that's all good, Sean.
Only it's my porn.

SPANK BANK

A HUGE ONE

MAGGIE: (O.S.) So — I guess it's back to the old spank bank for Mags.

SEAN: Wait a minute, honey. Sweetie. Did you just say spank bank?

MAGGIE: Yeah.

SEAN: Um — wow. You, um — you have a —

MAGGIE: Spank bank. Yes. A huge one. I know, I know — you probably think only men have spank banks but don't forget I grew up around Tommy — the king of the spank bank. I learned from the master how to store up eager little fantasies about tons of hot guys and then access them in my mind's eye whenever I felt the need to get off. (a beat) Haven't done it that way in ages, though. (she thinks for a second) Ooh. I can't wait. Don't you have to be somewhere?

WHO'S IN YOUR BANK?

NEEDLES: My wife's a snoop and I don't use computers and I HATE my wife and I got a shitload of romantic regrets so yeah — my spank bank's open every goddam day. I just put Helen Mirren in there. Not as The Queen. The other thing — the cop show from the BBC? Hot.

FRANCO: I usually have a rotating stable of a dozen or so women in my bank — famous chicks, chicks I save in fires, chicks I meet at my actual bank — that's my BANK spank bank but — since I met Natalie? It's only her in there. I might be in love.

LOU: Oh, an eclectic mix. Jessica Lange. Jessica Biel. Sally Field —

NEEDLES: Now or Gidget?

LOU: The Flying Nun.

SEAN: Scarlett Johansson. Rachel McAdams. Jennifer Aniston. Barbara Hirsch. Girl from high school. Brittany Klein — girl from high school. Karen Posnowski — high school.

TOMMY: Ellen DeGeneres. (off the reaction) Have you seen her dance?

KNOB JOB CAPITAL OF THE WORLD

TOMMY: How stupid can you be, Teddy? You don't go blowjob hunting on the boardwalk.

UNCLE TEDDY: Sure — tell me that now. Atlantic City has been ruined. Ruined! Couple years ago, it was the knob job capitol of the world. You couldn't not get a knob job. You'd get blown in the cab on the way in, you'd get blown getting the bags out of the trunk, blown on the way into the hotel —

DAD: Enough blowjob talk. I don't want the ball and chain finding out about this mess.

UNCLE TEDDY: Alright, alright. But I'm writing a letter to the Chamber of Commerce down there. I really am.

MAKE-UP SEX

DAD: The fights are incredible, but the make-up sex — let's just say I keep oxygen next to the bed.

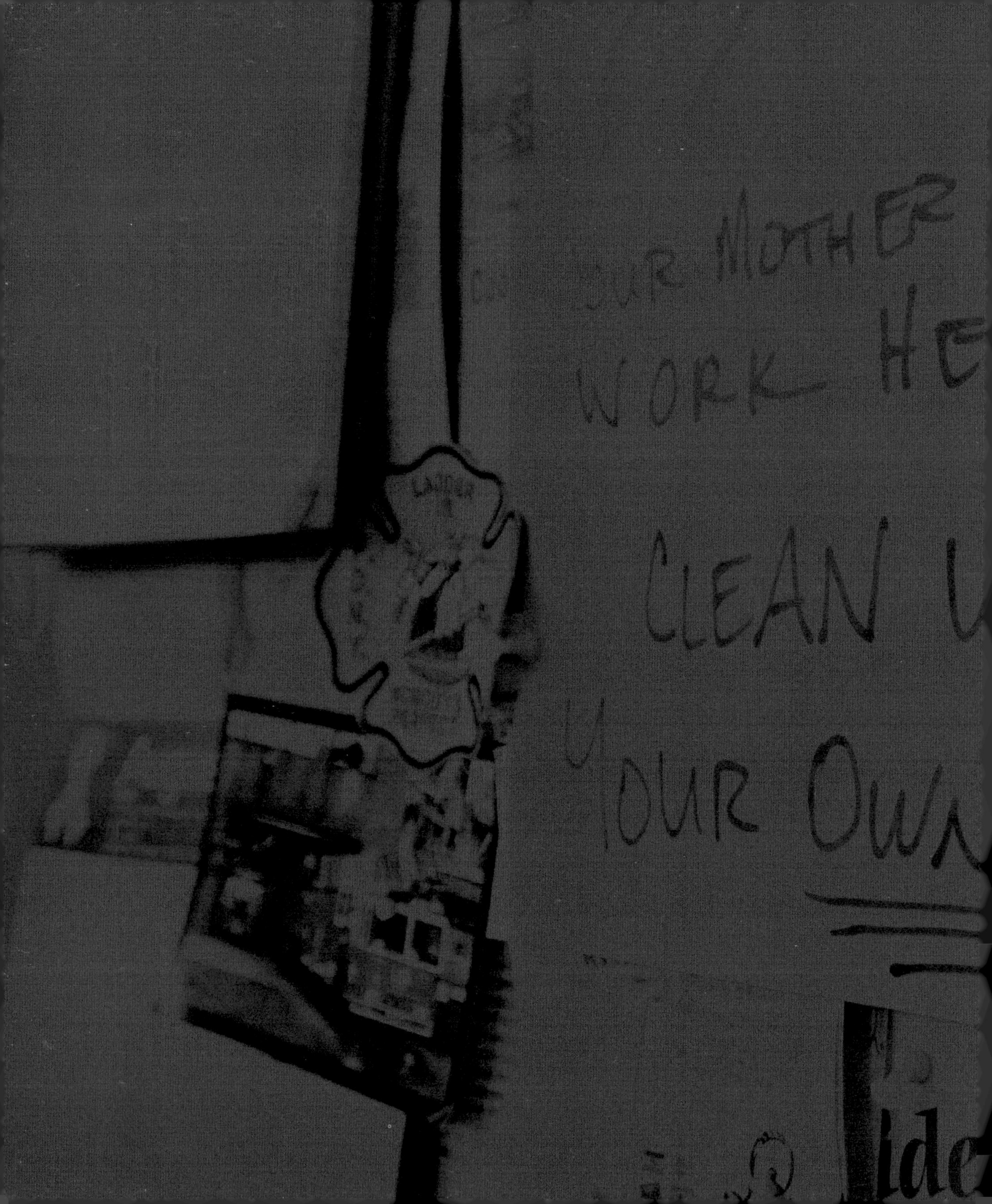
UR MOTHER
WORK HE
CLEAN U
OUR OWN
ide

DESN'T

E
!

CHAPTER 3

THE HOMO
STUFF

SAME SEX

TOMMY: Okay. What's with the fags these days? They're everywhere. Sitcoms, movies. Read in the paper about these same-sex marriages. They want to start doing them in New York.

JERRY: Same-sex marriages. Hey — right now I'd settle for a some-sex marriage.

THE GAYEST GUY IN THE CREW

TOMMY: You might slip in under the gay-dar. You being the queerest looking guy on the crew and all.

MIKE: Me? What about Sean?

TOMMY: Between the two, I'd have to say you win the Gayest Looking Guy on the Crew Contest. Hands down.

LOU: Or pants down, as the case may be.

SEAN: So, what — you're telling me his hair's better than mine? He's got a better body? What? C'mon

— look at the two of us and tell me I'm not gayer looking.

TOMMY: Hard to tell. Reach down and touch your toes.

GREAT EXPECTATIONS

Franco comes down the stairs.

FRANCO: What's goin' on?

LOU: *(explaining things)* This is the husband, this is the wood he barricaded the door with to keep us from saving his wife — who was in there on fire. This is what gay couples who insist on getting married have to look forward to.

FRANCO: Ain't love grand.

OTIS

JOHNNY: When you're in jail in some hick town taking it up the ass from Otis the drunk, don't call me. You'll be on your own.

TOMMY: No, I won't. I'll have Otis.

WHO'S A METROSEXUAL?

JERRY: What in the sweet chocolate Christ is a metrosexual?

MIKE THE PROBIE: It's — it means that you aren't gay but you like to do — certain things that might be — considered — gay. Right?

SEAN: No, asshole. He doesn't know what he's talking about. A metrosexual — is a, is a — straight guy who also happens to like to — go shopping and get — facials. 'N stuff.

TOMMY: Holy shit.

JERRY: *(not getting it)* Shopping for food?

MIKE THE PROBIE: Nice food.

SEAN: Yeah. And wine. And clothes. I'm not explaining it right. Franco — you know what a metrosexual is, right?

FRANCO: That would be a huge goddam no.

SEAN: *(to the others)* Look, it's not a gay thing. It's —

MIKE THE PROBIE: *(trying to help)* It's gay and it's not gay. It's

straight, regular guys getting facelifts and bikini waxes —

JERRY: Okay, that's it. Enough!

MIKE THE PROBIE: Male bikini waxes.

JERRY: *(roaring)* ENOUGH! From now on — nobody on this crew goes shopping for clothes unless they need underwear, winter boots or a goddam pair of gloves! And nobody — absolutely nobody — gets a facial unless that means washing the smoke off your face after a fire!

WHAT FLIPPED

JERRY: Uh-huh. So — nothing changed you. Your mother and I, we always had a good relationship when you were growing up. Sure there were fights every now and then, but that's normal. I used to grab her ass, you know, playing around — so it's not like I didn't lay the groundwork for you — guy-wise.

JERRY: Have your looks like

PETER: What are you saying?

JERRY: I'd hate to think — I mean, there's no way I did anything to make you turn — the way you are.

PETER: Gay.

JERRY: I mean, do you remember if — Okay, one time — you were real little. We got invited to a Halloween party. I didn't want to go, but your mother — she had to get out of the house. So we went — it was a costume party — and she made me dress up, which I definitely didn't want to do.

PETER: What did you go as?

JERRY: Sonny and Cher.

PETER: You must have made an interesting Sonny.

JERRY: That's not how it went down.

PETER: Oh, my God. You were Cher?

JERRY: Your mother wore a leisure suit and a fake moustache — I wore a wig and a dress. Maybe you saw us going out — maybe that's what flipped the switch.

PETER: No. I was born who I am, Dad. It's not your fault. Don't worry.

JERRY: I didn't think so.

PETER: But if you have any pictures of you as Cher —

JERRY: Shut up.

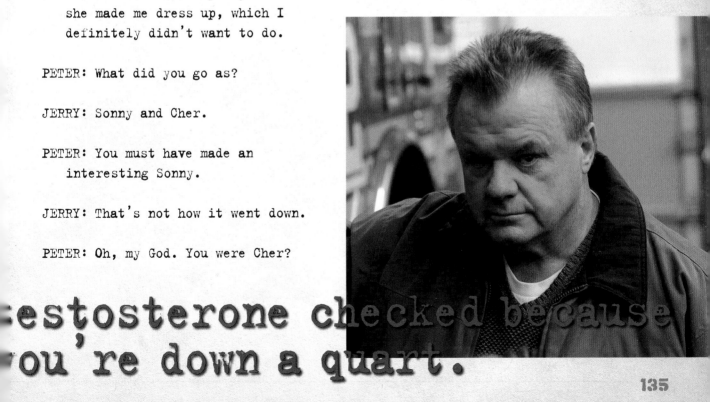

estosterone checked because ou're down a quart.

GAY AXE MURDERER

DAMIEN: You and my mother hooking up was kind of tough to deal with. Of course, now I'm living in Dyke Central, so who knows? I'll probably end up turning into some gay axe murderer or something.

TOMMY: Well, hopefully not gay.

PRO-LESBO

TOMMY: Shit. I wish my wife went lesbian on me. I'm pro-lesbian, brother. I am a large supporter of the lesbian community.

JIMMY: Really?

TOMMY: Hey — I'm a guy, you used to be a guy. We both know guys suck. You want your wife seeing some other horny, hungry, viagra-popping asshole with two gym bags full of secret DVD porn?

JIMMY: True. True. Where do you keep those gym bags, by the way?

TOMMY: Wasn't talking about me, asshole. Christ. Wish my daughter was a lesbian.

JIMMY: Which one?

TOMMY: Both. Too bad they don't have a pill for that.

THE BRIGHT SIDE

JANET: Your daughter is engaging in lesbian activity.

TOMMY: Honey, look on the bright side. Lesbians are big business right now. Ellen DeGeneres. Melissa Etheridge. Ninety-nine percent of the female golfing community.

AGAINST THE RULES

JANET: Colleen got suspended from school today for — get this — making out in the hallway.

TOMMY: That's against the rules now?

A TRAVESTY

COLLEEN: So I'm being honest. I have a girlfriend who I really, really, really like and who's really, really smart and we get in trouble for kissing in the hallway when there are kids like having sex in the stairwells? It's a joke.

TOMMY: It's a travesty. It's wrong.

COLLEEN: What — the me having a girl-friend thing or the kids having sex in the stairwells thing?

TOMMY: No no — the whole injustice thing. You should be free to be who you are — they shouldn't be persecuting you.

COLLEEN: Really?

TOMMY: Look — I love you, no matter what society or your mother or the government or anybody else says. You got to be who you were meant to be. That's why your grandparents came to this country — so you could be a lesbian, if that's what you wanted to be.

THE SAME UNDERLYING ENGINE

TOMMY: Nothing wrong with being gay.
No, sir. I used to think gay guys
had it made. You're a guy and
you're with a guy who has the same
interests as you. That's like a
win/win situation. First of all,
you both like to have a lot of
sex. Second of all, if you're both
interested in sports, you can go
to hockey games, basketball games,
football, baseball. It's all
blowjobs and ballgames.

JIMMY: Nah. Any long-term
relationship has the same
underlying engine. No matter what
the sexual affiliation might be.
Familiarity breeds contempt. You
fall in love, you move in together
'n then — after awhile — it's just
burning mutual resentment, ongoing
arguments over the division of the
household labor and secret evil
plans to piss the other person
off. It's a lot like Congress.
Or the Senate. Or the House of
Representatives.

CHAPTER 4

LOVE, MARRIAGE, BLAH...BLAH...BLAH

LOVE, MARRIAGE, BLAH, BLAH, BLAH

DON'T BEG

LAURA: Never going to happen.

SEAN: Did you not say you thought I was a nice person? And I was cute and in good shape? Did you not say those things?

LAURA: Yeah, well, that's exactly what I need — to get involved with one of the guys on my crew. That'll make life so much easier around here.

SEAN: Who said anything about getting involved? Drinks, dinner, maybe a movie —

LAURA: No.

SEAN: Please?

LAURA: Don't beg.

SEAN: Come on. You're neat.

LAURA: Oh, my God. Sean, I didn't bust my butt to get through probie school, then come here and eat shit on a daily basis so I could end up as your little girlfriend. That was never the goal, believe

it or not. I want the guys here to see me as a firefighter — nothing more, nothing less. I'm sorry.

SEAN: No, I get it. I get it. Yeah. Could we just make out a little?

HOW THIS IS GOING TO GO...

LAURA: Can I tell you how this is gonna go?

FRANCO: Please. I love a girl who takes charge.

LAURA: You'll beg and plead and whine and make cute little faces until I sleep with you, which I'll eventually do, of course, on account of you being a total stud and me being as unlaid as a pile of bricks.

FRANCO: I like it so far.

LAURA: Yeah, but — pretty soon I'll want more from the relationship — what with being a woman and all — and only because I'm so goddamn amazing in the sack, you'll actually try to commit for the first time in your life. You'll change for me, Franco, but you'll resent it real quick, and then I'll resent you for resenting me, and pretty soon we won't be able to stand being in the same room with each other, let alone forcing our body parts to intersect. But we'll have to be in the same room because we work together, which means unless one of us dies in a fire or moves away or kills the other one — we'll be forced to remember the hideous, bloody train wreck of a relationship that all started with your hand on my coat. Your move, stud.

FRANCO: *(a long beat)* See you tomorrow.

SEAN'S NEW CHICK

TOMMY: Hey probie — you know anything about Sean's new chick?

MIKE: Nah. He's been pretty tight-lipped. I know she's older.

FRANCO: How much older?

MIKE: Like a lot. She was watching Monday Night Football the night they announced John Lennon got shot.

FRANCO: So? That was 1980. Maybe she was only 5 years old.

MIKE: She had a bet on the game.

SHE'S SO DANGEROUS

FRANCO: Shit, Sean, there must be five million broads in this city — you got to pick Tommy's sister? Not to mention — she's insane. And I'm not saying insane like some judgment thing. I'm saying like the very serious mental disorder. She's a total whack job, dude.

SEAN: Yeah, but for me — she's perfect. She fits, you know? It's like — why I'm a firefighter. I go into a burning building, my heart's beating a mile a minute, I'm thinking, "I don't know if I'm getting out of this alive." That's how it is with her. Like she could just snap and take me out any second. She's so — dangerous.

SHE MAKES ME NERVOUS

MIKE: You doing anything? Want to go out, grab a beer?

SEAN: Maggie's coming by. We're going to take a walk, maybe get something to eat. You can join us —

MIKE: No, that's cool. You guys don't need me hanging around. Besides,

I like Maggie and everything, but she makes me nervous.

SEAN: Nervous how?

MIKE: Like if she looked at me for too long, I might cry.

SEAN: Yeah, I get that, too. But for me it's more hot than scary. Go figure.

COURTSHIP

MAGGIE: We got to find a place to eat. I'm starving. I had a Pop-Tart and two olives all day.

SEAN: Great diet, babe. This is nice, huh? Walking, feeling the cool air, doing a little window shopping. My parents used to do this a lot when they were courting. Just walk and look in the shop windows.

MAGGIE: Did you just say courting? Christ, what is this — Little House on the Goddamn Prairie?

SEAN: That's what people did back then. They courted.

MAGGIE: Yeah — and got diphtheria.

DON'T DO IT!

SEAN: Ow! I thought you weren't gonna hit me!

TOMMY: I'm not hitting you for banging my sister. I'm hitting you for being in love with her! Are you crazy?

SEAN: What?

TOMMY: All the chicks in the world, she's the one you're in love with? She's insane! She's been medicated since kindergarten — and maybe only once or twice in that whole time by someone other than herself. Run, don't walk.

SEAN: You're jealous.

TOMMY: I'm trying to protect you, numbnuts. If you went to the zoo and climbed into the bear exhibit and started poking it, I'd try and stop you, wouldn't I? Well, this is the same thing — only you don't have to go to the zoo and my sister's the bear and the stick's your cock. Don't do it!

TYING THE KNOT

SEAN: I got big news, bro. It concerns me and Mags.

LOU: You killed her.

SEAN: Quite the opposite. We're going to tie the knot.

LOU: So you'll kill her in three years.

TOMMY: If by tying the knot you mean making a noose with which to hang yourself then I'm all for it. If you mean tie the knot like you're marrying my sister — well, pretty much the same thing.

PROPOSAL

SEAN: The thing is, sir, my parents, they raised me right, I think, so I want to do things officially and in a respectful manner. So that's why I'm here — Mr. Gavin — to ask you most sincerely and most — something else — for your daughter Maggie's hand in marriage.

DAD: Are you retarded?

SEAN: Am I — ? No, sir. I've got some issues with reading comprehension —

DAD: What's the point of asking me for my daughter's hand after you've already asked her for it?

SEAN: Good point — Dad. Can I call you that? Or is it too soon?

DAD: I don't know. Is it too soon for me to call you asshole?

WEDDING ETIQUETTE

LOU: Do you applaud after a marriage in a graveyard?

TOMMY: Might as well. We're all going to hell anyway.

MARRIED LIFE

MIKE: So how's married life?

SEAN: Pretty good. Great, actually.
It's funny — I thought it was
going to be scary hooking up with
someone for the rest of my life,
but then I pulled the trigger
— it's fine. I'm totally okay
with it. I mean, I wake up in the
middle of the night shaking and I
pissed the bed a little one time
— but other than that —

MIKE: It's nice you got somebody.

RENEWAL

JANET: You know, have a little
ceremony, invite our friends and
family. Show the world we're still
devoted to each other.

TOMMY: Seems like a lot of work. Can't
we just get tattoos or something?

ULTIMATELY IT'S ABOUT THE RED SOX

DAD: I did the math. The way I
figured it, if I stayed with Teddy
— all the partying and whoring
— I'd be dead inside of two years.
If I stay with your mother, I
could last another ten. Ultimately
it's about the Red Sox. I'm not
sure they can win the World Series
in the next two years — but in the
next ten? There you have it.

149

MARRIAGE IS A BEAST, PART 1

JERRY: Marriage is a beast, boys. I've been at it for almost forty years. It's a beast whose claws and teeth get longer and sharper every goddam day. You want to fight back but you can't because if you do, the beast will break your spine in two. So you just — give in. You sit in front of the TV and sip your beer and hope to God she falls asleep first. Or that you die of a truly sudden and massive goddam heart attack.

MARRIAGE IS A BEAST, PART 2

LOU: My wife just flashes into my head now and then. Like a ten second nightmare.

CANDY: You miss her.

LOU: You spend twenty years with someone they're bound to leave their mark. Guess I miss the routine more than anything. Bad as things were at the end, there's still something to be said for a warm body lying next to you at night. Even if you can't stand to look her in the eye.

MARRIAGE IS A BEAST, PART 3

DAD: The last great woman I ever knew. Best years of my life I spent with her.

TOMMY: You fought like two wet cats in a bag.

DAD: Day to day it was rough. I admit that. But the years — wonderful.

YOU OLD FOOL

JEANNIE: Things may be muddled most of the time, but I'm clear in my mind when I tell you now that I love you. I love you despite all the things I hate about you. All the lousy, unspeakable things you've done, all your terrible flaws are forgiven. Did you hear me, you old fool? I love you.

LADDER

DATE	9X6	RIDING POSITION	TOOL ASSIG
LT. SHEA		OFF	LIFE
FF. JORGENSEN		LCC	HOO HALL
FF. GAVIN		OVM	HALL
FF. FRANCO RIVERA		ROOF	
FF. SEAN GARRITY		F/E	
FF. MIKE BOWER		CAN	

CHAPTER 5

WE ARE FAMILY

SHE'S PUERTO RICAN, MAN

FRANCO: I got a kid at home. A Puerto Rican kid. Her mom was a spick. I'm a spick. She's going to be stuck in NYC public schools for like the next goddam decade unless I do something about it. I'd like her to go to the best private schools in the city — with wealthy white kids — schools where they don't stab or kill each other but they just do really good drugs and get incredible grades and then go to great white colleges and do even better drugs and then graduate with well-connected white friends who get them hired into the upper echelons of white American society. Those schools average out at between 15 grand a year now and ultimately — in college — almost 50K a pop.

If I got a little money to start I'm hoping the whole 'her dad's a fireman' angle will help push us over the top when it comes to some financial aid and then — if I'm a lieutenant making almost fifty grand a year TOTAL — hey — between me and the federal government — maybe I can pull it off.

She's Puerto Rican, man. She's also a girl. With no Mom. I need to do her a solid.

TOMMY: Right. You know there was an article in New York magazine last month about blow job contests in the NYC prep schools. The girls got points for —

FRANCO: Yeah, yeah. I read it. Guess I hope my daughter has a shot at winning one of those.

FAMILY VALUES

TOMMY: Hey, guys. Morning.

CONNOR: Katy failed her spelling test.

KATY: I studied really hard.

TOMMY: That's okay, sweetie. I failed plenty of tests and look at me. (to Connor) What kind of brother are you, ratting out your sister? No Gameboy for a week.

CONNOR: But Dad —

TOMMY: No buts.

CONNOR: Can we get a dog?

TOMMY: Bad time to ask. Start picking your spots better.

WHAT IS HITLER?
WHAT IS SPERM?

KATY: Who's Hitler?

TOMMY: What?

KATY: Uncle Lou's making us watch a show about him and the Jews.

TOMMY: (calling off) Lou?

LOU: (off camera) It's educational! These kids need some learning!

KATY: What's sperm?

TOMMY: It's a — food thing. Like Spam — only spelled differently. And it's harder to find in the stores.

KATY: I thought sperm was the stuff

that comes out of the man's penis during intercourse.

TOMMY: What the hell are you teaching these kids? (to Katy) Go learn about the Jews.

HOW A BRIBE WORKS

TOMMY: Who's your Mom seeing?

COLLEEN: I can't tell you.

TOMMY: Isn't there something in the bible about honoring your mother and father? I think Jesus wants me to know who your mother's seeing.

COLLEEN: Yeah, but if I tell you, I'll be dishonoring her — so I really can't.

TOMMY: Okay — what about all the clothes you just got? That doesn't count for anything?

COLLEEN: Dad, when you want information, you ask first, then you offer the bribe. That's how it works. You did it the wrong way around this time.

155

VACATION

JOHNNY: Where do you want to go on vacation?

KATY: Disney World.

COLLEEN: Jerusalem.

JOHNNY: Jerusalem? Jesus. Sorry. I got it. Miami Beach. More Jews per square inch than the entire country of Israel. Times ten.

COLLEEN: Whatever. Like this family would ever be allowed into the Holy Land. They've probably got our pictures pasted on the wall at the airport.

JOHNNY: You say that like it's a bad thing.

WHAT DAD DOES

KATY: I like Uncle Johnny. He's so nice. He never gets mad. He never yells at us. And he never does that thing that dad does where he says something and then a few seconds later has to explain that he didn't mean what he just said.

JANET: Oh. You mean sarcasm.

RESTLESS

ANGIE: Sheel told me about you and Janet and you and her — and Johnny and Janet. Jesus, throw in a brain tumor, maybe an evil twin, it's like an episode of "The Young and the Restless."

A NORMAL FAMILY

JANET: Now go and pray for a more normal family if you think it will help.

COLLEEN: The Lord can only do so much.

GAVIN FAMILY TRAITS

TOMMY: And you know what else? Colleen is having sex now, too.

JANET: I know. That's why I got her on the pill.

TOMMY: You — you got her — Jesus Christ — okay, great. When did I — of all people — become the moral compass in this family? And when were you planning on telling me about all this?

JANET: What — the sex?

TOMMY: The sex — pills? Yeah. Drugs, the booze — All of it.

JANET: Okay. I was going to drop the sex bomb on you a while ago, but our plutonic living arrangement has been going so well, and you always hear the word "sex" as an invitation, so I didn't want to risk it. As for the pot and booze, check her birth certificate. The last name is Gavin.

FEMALE GAVIN

TOMMY: She's a female Gavin. Expressing emotion goes on pretty much non-stop twenty-four/seven, even in her sleep.

IN ROCK 'N ROLL YEARS

COLLEEN: He's the lead singer.

TOMMY: The musicians are the four guys standing behind him. Lead singer that's the guy who wears make up and does all the drugs and bangs a different girl every night. How old is this Tony guy?

COLLEEN: Twenty-six.

TOMMY: Twenty-six. Jesus Christ. Twenty six and he's a lead singer? You know how old that is in rock 'n roll years? Seventy. He's Clint Eastwood.

THE BABY HATES ME

TOMMY: Oh Jesus — are you going to do the postpartum thing again, because I'll book a room somewhere until it passes.

JANET: It's not postpartum. That baby hates me.

TOMMY: He's too young to hate.

JANET: He's half-Gavin. He was born to hate. Come to think of it — he might be all-Gavin. Half you, half Johnny.

OUR FAMILY IN A NUTSHELL

JOHNNY: Before you do anything — not that I have any idea what that anything would be — stop and do something you'll find completely foreign. Think. We just found

TOMMY: A lot of adopted kid

out our father was banging some
strange broad for thirty plus
years, we've got a priest brother
and a former DQ employee sister
floating around out there, now our
old man's living on Park Avenue
with Yoko Ono's grandmother, not
to mention the whole you-knocking-
up-our-dead-cousin's-wife thing.
That's our family in a nutshell.

WE GAVINS

TOMMY: We Gavins are a passionate
   tribe. We settle our grievances
   the Irish way, know what I mean?

SEAN: Sure.

TOMMY: No you don't because you're
   modern Irish. Your generation
   likes to think about things, then
   talk them out. My generation, we
   feel things then beat them out of

each other. That goes back to the
old country. Back in Ireland my
grandfather nearly killed his best
friend with a rock for flirting
with my grandma. Kid lived, but
he was never the same.

THE USUAL

TEDDY: How was your day, sunshine?

TOMMY: The usual combination of
   misery, blackness and self-hatred.

EVERY FAMILY HAS ONE

FRANCO: You got a cousin who's a
   sculptor?

TOMMY: Every family has that one
   black sheep right? Most families
   get a retard — we got a sculptor.
   Same thing really.

urn out all right.
Look at Courtney Love.

BROTHER STUFF

JOHNNY: You know, what happened last night, that's just brother stuff.

KATY: Me and Connor never fought like that.

JOHNNY: Yeah, but it's different with two boys. Especially grown up boys. We can be a pretty dopey bunch sometimes.

KATY: Why?

JOHNNY: I'm not sure. It's like — you got any slow kids at your school, honey?

KATY: You mean the special ed class. Miss Lane says we shouldn't call them slow.

JOHNNY: And she's absolutely right. I meant special eds. Your dad and me, we're special eds when it comes to dealing with — feelings and emotions — that kind of garbage. Doesn't make us bad people, we're just not — equipped like everyone else. You get me?

She shakes her head, "no."

JOHNNY: (cont'd) You will some day.

BROTHERS AND SISTERS

MAGGIE: We always had a special bond, me and you. Backed each other up.

TOMMY: I know, I know.

MAGGIE: Sometimes I think the only reason you like me is because I'm the one person the family hates more than you.

TOMMY: Well, there may be a sliver of truth to that. But I love you, Mags. Johnny loves you.

MAGGIE: Don't pump sunshine up my ass, Tom. Johnny's scared shitless of me. Always was. Uncle Teddy tolerates me. It's obvious how Daddy feels. I know I'm no saint. I'm spiteful, angry, untrustworthy, hateful, dishonest — just like Dad. But I'm trying to change. Remember what Mommy used to say?

TOMMY: Stay out of my liquor cabinet?

GAVIN CLEANING TIPS

JANET: It still smells like puke in here.

TOMMY: I used the Glade.

JANET: Did you use the Suddenly Spring or the Delicate Petals because the Suddenly Spring is better for puke and the Delicate Petals is for everything else.

A MILLION YEARS OR SO

JANET: Tommy, you don't know Roger. He would never do something like that. Not in a million years.

TOMMY: Why do people say that? It's not like we're gonna have a million years to find out for sure.

TOMMY: Once you piss o

a guy, where can you go?

WHEN A WOMAN LIES

LOU: Doesn't make sense.

TOMMY: You're telling me.

LOU: You got all kinds of questions here. Why did she lie about talking to this O'Brien guy?

TOMMY: And what's she really doing with the money?

LOU: That, too. It's troubling. I mean, when a man lies —

TOMMY: It's meaningless.

LOU: Completely.

TOMMY: We're genetically engineered to lie.

LOU: It's like breathing. In with the air, out with the lie.

TOMMY: It's a time-saver, really. Think of all the long, drawn-out idiotic conversations you'd have to have if you told the truth all the time. Lying eliminates tension, conflict —

LOU: High blood pressure.

TOMMY: Not to mention cholesterol. All kinds of bad things.

LOU: Unless you get caught.

TOMMY: Right.

LOU: But when a woman lies —

TOMMY: That's bad. And Janet — she never lies.

LOU: Never?

TOMMY: She's a freak of nature that way.

DIVORCE POOL

TOMMY: There's a pool on my divorce?

JERRY: (offended) No. (a beat) Yes. Look — I give you the tour off, you give me the odds.

TOMMY: I'd say — 60/40. Divorce.

NO MORE YAPPING!

INT. BROWNSTONE/2ND FLOOR APARTMENT
A SMALL MAN in his early seventies is standing in front of a door. He wears thick glasses and walks with the aid of a cane. He has a hammer in one hand and there are several pieces of wood hammered across the door.

SMALL MAN: You can go now. Everything's fine. I was just making toast.

TOMMY: Well, this is interesting.

Sean has joined the guys with a hose as Tommy and Billy pry the wood off the door. Lou holds the old man a few feet away.

LOU: Sir, why would you nail the door there shut? If this is related to your burning toast story, I'm not seeing the connection. Did you do that to keep the toast inside? Did it become violent when you burned it? Help us out.

SMALL MAN: You can't go in there. Not yet.

TOMMY: We have to check the room, sir. We've been told there's a woman missing.

SMALL MAN: She's not missing. She's right where I left her — on the couch, soaked in kerosene.

LOU: You see? If Dr. Phil wasn't so busy, things like this wouldn't happen.

TOMMY: You want to tell us why you'd do such a thing?

SMALL MAN: Fifty-two years I put up with her yapping! Fifty-two goddam years! And then she started in today and I said to myself, today's the day. From now on — no more yappin'!

LOU: Well, let's see, hundreds of dollars for marriage counseling, or a buck fifty for a gallon of gas. I see where you're coming from, sir.

CHAPTER 6

RELIGION

GOD'S PLAN?

Forget 9/11. Five years ago? Black kid. Ten years old. I grab him from inside a closet. Hot fire — all around. He's burned — scared — slipping and sliding around in my arms like a goddam baby seal — got him almost all the way out when his skin — kid's wearing underwear and nothing else — we're one flight away from making it outside safe and sound and, uh — his skin comes off like — wrapping on a Christmas present. Slips right out of my arms and falls on the floor. Pick him up, take him outside, three months later he dies in the burn center.

Three years ago — project fire six stories up — one-bedroom apartment with fifteen people living in it — I find a little girl under a couch — she's holding a kitten. Carry them both out — six stories — switching off my mask between me and her and the goddam kitten for six goddam stories and the whole way down she's crying up at me about the kitten. Please save my kitten Mr. Fireman. Don't let anything happen to my kitten Mr. Fireman. I'm biting my tongue 'cause I hate cats. I think they suck. I'm from a dog family. Anyways. Long story short. Cat lived. She didn't.

9/11, I lost four good men including my cousin Jimmy, my best friend — you want to talk about that? Best goddam fireman I ever worked with. Good family man, dedicated American, blah blah blah. Every day I drive to work, I drive through my neighborhood and see guys, drunken assholes I went to high school with who stand on the corner high, and I gotta wonder why these assholes are still walking around and Jimmy Keefe ain't? My cousin the priest says it's all part of God's plan. Apparently — God's got a plan. Well let me tell you something. If there is a God? He's got a whole shitload of explaining to do.

— **Tommy Gavin**

BLIND

JESUS CHRIST: You have to hold onto some hope Tommy. Some faith.

TOMMY: Sorry pal. No hope. All out. Tank's empty.

JESUS CHRIST: You play the eye for an eye game — pretty soon every one ends up blind.

EX-PRIEST

TOMMY: They kick you out of the priesthood or did you just retire?

MICKEY THE PRIEST: Little a both. Look — only time you ever call me is when you're in a tough spot and you want to bullshit about God and guilt and blah blah blah so what is it this time? Booze? Broads? You got prostate cancer? What?

TOMMY: Nice.

MICKEY THE PRIEST: So it ain't cancer.

MINOR COMMANDMENTS

KATY: Daddy, do you believe in the ten commandments?

TOMMY: Well — I've broken a few of them myself. The more minor ones. I felt bad about doing that so — yeah. I guess I do.

TWELVE STEPS TO ANGELINA

INT. REC CENTER — NIGHT
Mike is off chatting with a young lady. Sean is immersed in conversation with the Meeting Leader.

SEAN: These meetings have really had an impact on me, you know? I mean, the whole idea of the eight steps —

MEETING LEADER: Twelve steps.

SEAN: Twelve — right. Twelve steps. And all the stuff about moral categories —

MEETING LEADER: Taking a moral inventory.

SEAN: That's what I mean. It's just been like a total awakening for me. But I guess it's the whole God thing that's got me stuck. Never been a fan.

MEETING LEADER: Well, you should think of God in terms of however it is you understand Him — or Her.

SEAN: Her? You mean God could be a chick?

MEETING LEADER: If that's how you perceive God.

SEAN: Yeah, oh yeah. My God would totally be a chick. Can I put a face to it? . . . Angelina Jolie. That's my God right there.

MEETING LEADER: Well, then — Angelina — would probably tell you that you are powerless over your disorder. And that no human power can relieve the problem.

SEAN: So, she'll help me fix it.

MEETING LEADER: Yes. But first you have to stop thinking so selfishly. You must turn your will and your life over to Her.

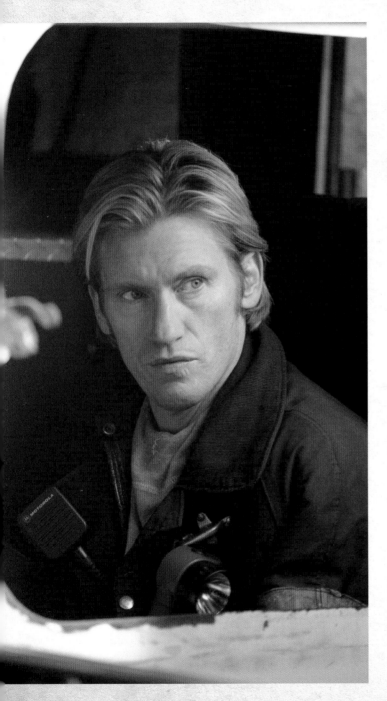

SEAN: To Angelina.

MEETING LEADER: Yes.

SEAN: Not a problem.

NO HEAVEN

KATY: I believe there's no heaven, just like there's no God. Human beings made those things up so they can feel special — more special than the animals or bugs. Because we're scared. We need to think there's someone out there protecting us — watching over us. We're nothing. We come from dirt and we go back into the dirt.

REMEMBER LIMBO?

INT. CATHOLIC CHURCH — NIGHT
Sean is kneeling at the altar.

SEAN: Um — look, I'm a little — confused. I know, I'm confused most of the time but now I'm like super confused. When I was a kid it was simple — there was heaven and then there was hell. If you were good you went upstairs and if you were bad you went the other way but if you were an innocent little kid or a baby who choked on something or something you went to limbo. Remember limbo? Then you guys cancelled limbo. But now I got a dead kid on my hands and another kid — a live kid who says there is no heaven, just — dirt. Apparently. So, I don't know. I'm getting all these mixed messages. I figure best thing to do is go right to the source, so — think you could help me out here? *(a beat)* I'll wait.

GO TO HELL

TOMMY: You a Muslim?

CABBIE: Yes.

TOMMY: You really believe when you die and go to — whatever — you get 77 virgins.

CABBIE: 72.

TOMMY: Virgins. What a waste of time.

CABBIE: What are you?

TOMMY: I'm nothing. Lapsed Catholic.

Organized religion is bullshit.

CABBIE: Well my friend — you are going to hell! All Godless Americans! You will burn in hell. With your sex and drugs and your rock music!

TOMMY: Oh yeah? Well I'd rather go to hell. Where they have 72 whores! Whores who give hand jobs and head and Elvis is there and so is John Lennon and all we do is party our Goddamn asses off! You can stick your stupid Goddamn virgins in your filthy Goddamn head-rag shit for brains!

HOPE IS KICKING MY ASS...

TOMMY: Thing is Mick — when we were kids? This place meant something, y'know? The cross, the rituals, the music? It was like no matter what we did wrong, no matter how bad things were out there in the world — how many wars there were, how many Charlie Mansons, how many Kennedys they killed — coming here, every Sunday morning for an hour — that would somehow make everything turn out alright.

MICKEY: Tom, I don't know what you want me to say.

TOMMY: I want you to say that it's all bullshit. That there's no map, there's no plan. There's no golden ring at the end of the ride. We're just a slightly more civilized version of the animal kingdom. We're lions. With clothes and booze and satellite dishes. That's all.

TOMMY: Take away the hope, Mick. That's what I really want you to do. Because of the Big Three — Faith, Hope and Charity? The one that's dragging me down every day — the one that's kicking my ass — is Hope. It's making me think I can fix my marriage. I can't do the math anymore, man. Take away Jimmy, take away Joey Fuller, but keep the crackhead who wants to kill the fireman who's trying to save his life? Let the Murphy kid walk away from this accident, but send my little girl — my baby — to the hospital? All this stuff's happening, but I'm supposed to hold out hope?

MICKEY: Yes. Yes you are. Because in the end? Hope is all we got left.

NOSEBLEEDS

MAGGIE: Sean, I get within three blocks of a church I get nosebleeds. I literally hemorrhage from my face. No goddamn churches.

RUMORS

COLLEEN: Grampa, did I tell you how much Jesus loves you?

DAD: Yeah, sweetheart, a couple of times. Tell Jesus to keep it to himself. I'm glad he loves me, but that's how rumors get started.

DINNER WITH A NUN

TOMMY: That's fine, but you don't surprise people with this kind of shit — dinner with a nun. You got to prepare for a nun dinner. You got to be in the right place mentally. Have a bunch of stuff picked out to talk about in advance — stuff that's clean. I can't come up with that kind of stuff on the spot. I stopped thinking clean years ago. Give me five minutes. Tell her I needed to

DO-OVER

TOMMY: All that shit I said
    about God over the years?

LOU: Yeah.

TOMMY: I take most of it back.

get some air or something. I'll think of things we can discuss — Vatican II, the Holy Ghost — shit, what else?

BIBLE PARTS

JIMMY: This reminds me of Sister Mary Gregory back in school. Remember what she always used to say? "Revenge is the poor delight of little minds."

TOMMY: You're throwing Sister Mary Gregory at me? Whose side are you on?

JIMMY: I'm just saying — two wrongs don't make a right.

TOMMY: Hey, this is in the Bible, okay?

JIMMY: Thou shalt have your ex-wife's boyfriend falsely arrested?

TOMMY: Exodus. "An eye for an eye, a tooth for a tooth."

JIMMY: Like you know the Bible.

TOMMY: I know the parts I can use.

MAGIC

MICKEY: Don't tell me you all of a sudden believe in God — the Catholic version of God that we were raised with — again.

TOMMY: No. I believe in — those candles. Y'know the whole David Copperfield David Blaine aspect of the Catholic church?

MICKEY: Fill me in.

TOMMY: The resurrection, the immaculate conception, the Jesus feeding ten thousand people with one loaf a bread and a fish, the walking on water thing, the whole magic aspect? That stuff use to make me laugh my ass off. But now? I got to say — I kind of buy it. It's magic. God makes things disappear. And I'm fine with that. Sometimes it's living breathing good strong honest people. And sometimes — it's ghosts.

THAT NEW CAR SMELL

TEDDY: Don't you love that new car smell? I'm thinking of having it

pumped into my casket when I die.
I'll get to heaven, God will take
me by the hand, he'll say, "You
really don't deserve to be up
here, Ted, but I just had to get
a whiff of you!"

I FOUND HIM

TOMMY: Hey — you know how people —
religious people — are always asking
you — 'have you found Jesus'?

MICKEY: Uh-huh.

TOMMY: I did. I found him, Mick.

MICKEY: Oh yeah? Where's He been for
the last two thousand years?

TOMMY: Apparently my new apartment.

Mickey darkens a little. Tommy leans in.

TOMMY: He's been — showing up. On the
cross, off the cross. Half-off the
cross. One time He even showed up
on the ceiling of Sheila's kitchen.
What do you think THAT means?

MICKEY: Sheila needs to get a new
decorator.

A GOD COMPLEX

MICKEY: What — like you don't have a
God complex?

TOMMY: Hey — I run into burning
buildings to save people God
apparently doesn't give a shit
about. I guess He's too busy
helping Terrell Owens catch ten
passes in the Super Bowl and
making sure P. Diddy makes twenty
five million off half-assed hip hop
records and designer baggy pants.

MICKEY: Why don't you ask Jesus why
His Dad lets that happen?

TOMMY: We don't really talk.

JESUS

JESUS CHRIST: That wasn't my mom.
That was my girlfriend. Mary
Magdalene. She hates my guts.
Well — she loves me AND she hates
me. I was never home I was always
out with the guys I never took
her anywhere, blah blah blah. I
don't have to tell YOU about that
bullshit. Broads. You making me a
sandwich or what?

CHAPTER 7
GHOSTS AND HEROES

IT'S THE GHOSTS, TOMMY

DAD: My father cried a lot near the end of his life. He never cried before then, probably not even as a baby — but those last few years, you'd look at him cross-eyed and he'd bust out bawling. It's the ghosts, Tommy.

TOMMY: What do you mean?

DAD: All the people you hurt, all the mistakes you made. You get old, you stop moving a million miles a minute — it all comes back. It finally catches up with you. And all you can do is cry.

IS THIS MY FINAL RESTING PLACE?

TOMMY: Had another dead person talk to me — Asian girl. West Side Highway.

JIMMY: So the starting to drink again thing's working out well, hah? What'd she say?

TOMMY: Please, sir. I want to go home.

JIMMY: Join the club, kid.

TOMMY: What's that supposed to mean?

JIMMY: Hey! Put yourself in my shoes. I'm supposed to spend eternity arguing with you about your secret evil plans to fix your failing marriage? This can't be my final resting place.

TOMMY: What if it is?

JIMMY: What if? What if I'm not really here? What if I'm just a figment of your imagination?

TOMMY: If you were a figment of my imagination you wouldn't be arguing with me, you'd be helping me to solve the problems here.

JIMMY: Which one? The wife problem? The drinking problem? The ghost thing?

TOMMY: Very funny.

JIMMY: Y'know what? Maybe I'm an element of your subconscious. Maybe I'm here because you don't even know why I'm here. Yet.

GHOST MAGNET

SHEILA: So I was talking to Lisa last night, my friend the psychic. She said she — she thinks you might be a — ghost magnet. She's really, really empowered Tommy she is almost never wrong and she said she got a vibe from you that —

TOMMY: What vibe? I don't have a vibe. I can't afford a vibe. Jesus Christ.

SHEILA: Look — she said people like you are — open vessels, you're —

TOMMY: Yeah yeah — I'm a vessel. I'm a boat! I'm a goddam ship full of goddam ghosts.

SHEILA: She said you are prone to — visits. Visitations I think she said. She felt like Jimmy was close to you.

This shit is freaking Tommy out because it's so right on the money.

TOMMY: I — I dunno what she's — she's smoking something cause I — I'm a magnet I'm a vessel I'm a mess is what I am Jesus Christ. What?

SHEILA: (*dead straight*) Have you seen Jimmy?

TOMMY: (*unprepared*) No.

SHEILA: Tommy — don't lie to me. You know how much it means to me. Look me straight in the eye and tell me you haven't seen him.

TOMMY: I have not seen Jimmy. You know how much it would mean to me if I could. I am not a magnet I am not a ship —

SHEILA: Vessel —

TOMMY: — whatever. I'm me. Just me.

I SEE DEAD PEOPLE....

DOCTOR: Don't tell me you're seeing dead people.

TOMMY: Maybe.

DOCTOR: Are you really seeing dead people?

TOMMY: Yeah.

DOCTOR: Nobody told you to say that?

TOMMY: No.

DOCTOR: Because word's gone around that seeing dead people's an automatic two-week vacation. I got three, four guys a week coming in here with the dead people story. It's like I'm living that movie with the kid who sees dead people. What's that kid's name? He's good.

WHO ELSE CAN I BLAME?

TOMMY: I blame the system — the schools hire these freaky broads — they ought to have a better screening process.

JIMMY: That's funny. 'Cause I blame you.

TOMMY: Why me?

JIMMY: Because I'm dead. Who the hell else am I gonna blame?

FAITH IN HUMANITY

LOU: Come on, Tom. Where's your
    faith in humanity?

TOMMY: Buried somewhere on the
    southern tip of Manhattan.

HOW TO HANDLE SURVIVOR'S GUILT

TODD: I knew eight guys down at Ground Zero. One of them was my first partner. Guy who showed me how the job worked. Took me under his wing. I had to give the eulogy at his funeral mass. I started getting the survivor's guilt about three days after we buried him.

TOMMY: Shit. What did you do about it? You talk to somebody or something?

TODD: My dad. His partner — his best friend — got shot on a drug bust twenty years ago. My dad kicked in this door, ducked the shots. Partner took two in the dome. So — I figured he'd be the guy to turn to. Find out how he coped, you know?

TOMMY: Yeah. What did he have to say?

TODD: Zilch. Cracked me one in the face and told me to suck it up. Walk it off, he says. ... Eventually I got a handle on it. On my own.

TOMMY: How?

TODD: Booze. I drank — a lot. Still do. I mean not on the job or anything, and I'm not drunk right now, but I will be pretty soon. Like — right after this. Dozen beers and six tequilas. That'll pretty much knock it right out of yer system.

TOMMY: Okay, then. Thanks for the advice.

TODD: No problem. You wanna go for one? Talk some more?

TOMMY: I better not. I'm on the wagon.

Todd laughs out loud.

TODD: Sorry. Good luck with that.

ABOUT THE SPOTLIGHT

EXT. BAR — NIGHT
As the crew heads for their cars, the overwhelming glow of Manhattan's downtown skyline overtakes them. They gather into an unplanned group and stare at it.

JERRY: Remember when they had those two spotlights? Right after 9/11? Shooting straight up into the sky? That was too much for me. I like it like this. Empty. Just like those scumbags left it. No spotlights, no new buildings — just empty.

Everyone stares out at it, their faces a mix of loss, regret and anger.

TOMMY: That's the thing about the spotlight — you walk out into it, and at first everybody sees a big, tall good-looking handsome American hero. You stay in the spotlight long enough — pretty soon they start to notice you have a scar on your upper lip. And one eye's bigger than the other. And your nose is a little crooked. And so are your teeth. After a while — you start to look like a goddamn monster. Like goddamn King Kong. And then they start to throw shit at you. Let me tell you something — that morning — they threw a couple of jets into a couple of buildings. But they also threw the biggest job in the history of this profession at us. And what did we do? We gave up 343 lives so that at least — at least — ten thousand others could be saved. I'll take those odds any goddamn day of the week. But three miserable years later what are we doing? Still waiting for a goddamn raise. We're on our own, kids. We're always gonna be on our own.

COMPLICATED

TOMMY: Look — I got twenty years on the job. I was there 9/11 —

The cop holds up a very experienced and tired hand.

COP: You know, it really ticks me off when people use a tragedy to excuse certain behaviors — such as parking illegally. 9/11 was four years ago, champ. Get over it.

Tommy doesn't know how to react.

COP: You had your day. They wrote books about you guys — big, giant coffee-table size books with glossy pictures. They made that John Travolta movie about you, put you up on a pedestal — and

what happened? Turns out you ain't just heroes. Turns out some of you do blow and have gang bangs. Turns out some of you are just broken-down drunks on the verge of a complete and total mental collapse.

That last line hits Tommy pretty hard.

COP: *(cont'd)* America don't like it when things get complicated, pal.

START WITH BIG FAT DEAD GUYS

EXT. MANHATTAN STREET — DAY
Franco, Sean, Laura, Lou and Tommy exit what was a false alarm.

JERRY: Everything all right in there?

LOU: Big fat dead guy in a bathtub.

JERRY: How fat?

LOU: Kirstie Alley fat actress fat.

TOMMY: Elvis at the end fat.

JERRY: Jesus.

TOMMY: He left the water running. Been dead since yesterday afternoon. Flooded the first three floors.

JERRY: Suicide?

LOU: Let's put it this way — the note said 'Tell my wife I hope she's happy now.'

TOMMY: God knows he is.

JERRY: So —

LOU: We turned the faucet off and told the super to call the cops.

TOMMY: Our work here is done.

LOU: Hey — they want to run point on terrorist attacks? Let 'em start with the big fat dead guys.

FAULT LINES

TOMMY: It wasn't your fault. Five, six times a year I got to deal with what ifs and I shouldas and maybe I could've. Christ. 9/11. I got a million regrets wrapped in ten million shoulda, oughtas from that morning alone.

NO GUARANTEES

LOU: — after 9/11. After our four guys — and the other fifty-two guys I knew — fifty-two guys. Fifty-two guys I came out of the academy with, spent two or ten years working with, was best man at their marriage or godfather to their kids with — with, with, with! What I think?

What I think is — everybody should do whatever the hell they want and they should do a goddamn lot of it right now — because tomorrow ain't no guarantee.

Birth, school, work, death. It goes that quick.

MEMORIAL

The 9/11 memorial outside the house — a beautifully crafted bronze memorial of the tragedy, listing all 343 names of the fallen. The guys stand together quietly, taking it in. Mike steps forward and points out a few names.

MIKE: Here's Jimmy. Bobby.

FRANCO: I read about this in the Times. The picture didn't do it justice.

LOU: You realize this is here because firefighters and normal people wanted to honor the guys we lost. There were no politicians involved. You get those pricks involved, you're left with what they got over at Ground Zero — two big, empty goddamn holes. I feel for all the families over there waiting for a memorial for their loved ones. Because we already got ours.

SEAN: I hear the mayor didn't even come to the dedication.

TOMMY: I was here that day. Before they installed it, the guys in this house — they lost a lot of brothers in the towers — they wrote personal messages, prayers, remembrances — on the back. Then they sealed it up so nobody will ever see what they wrote.

LOU: That's how it should be. It stays between brothers.

FRANCO: Each other is all we got, right?

EPISODE GUIDES
WITH MUSIC PLAYLISTS

SEASON 1

1: GAY

Amidst Tommy's recurring nightmares, the men of 62 Truck are taken aback by a newspaper interview in which retiring fireman Bobby Teff announces that he and at least twenty of the men who died on 9/11 are gay. While Jerry cannot keep his anger in check, the men under his command try to come to grips with the fact that there could be gay firemen, perhaps even somebody in their firehouse. Meanwhile, following a chance encounter with Roger, Tommy uses his godson Damian's computer skills to disrupt the life of Janet's new boyfriend. And after promising to check up on his late cousin Jimmy's widow, Sheila, Tommy is stunned when his eavesdropping finds her with another woman.

During a brownstone fire started by a frustrated husband setting his nagging wife on fire, Mike is credited with saving his first life in the line of duty. Unable to shake his concern over the news that there may be gay firefighters in their midst, Jerry continues to ask around about Bobby Teff. And when he tracks the newly retired fireman down at his favorite bar, he loses control in an angry attack that leaves Teff in a coma. Meanwhile, as Roger struggles with the fallout from a computer virus at work and some mysteriously cancelled credit cards, Tommy is unable to stay in the shadows while trailing Sheila and her friend, Lisa, at the supermarket. So, during his next visit with Jimmy's ghost, Tommy says that his widow could be a lesbian.

As trouble brews for Jerry following his attack on Teff, Tommy cannot contain himself any longer and confronts Janet about her plans to move to California with Roger. Despite Tommy's pleas to stay somewhere nearby so that he can continue to see their children, Janet is adamant about wanting to get far away from the pall of death that has been hanging over NYFD's men and their families since 9/11. Finally, as Mike doesn't know what to make of the display of gratitude he's received from the man whose life he saved, Tommy looks for relief from his troubles in booze and easy sex.

Directed by: John Fortenberry

Written by: Peter Tolan & Denis Leary

Music: "Don't Panic" by Coldplay, "Stronger Than Dirt" By Tom McRae

2: KANSAS

As Jerry faces an investigation into his beating of gay firefighter Bobby Teff, the annual ice hockey game against the police has put Tommy at odds with his gruff co-captain, Ryan. Though pleased with his campaign of harassment against Janet's boyfriend, when his godson, Damian, threatens to reveal how he infected Roger's computer with a virus, Tommy is forced to pay $500 for his silence. Making matters worse, when he is unable to avoid his late cousin's wife, Sheila, Tommy learns that Ryan has asked her on a date. Meanwhile, as Mike struggles with the attentions of the man whose life he saved, and Lou is asked to read his poetry to a 9/11 survivors support group, Jerry is told to look for eyewitnesses who will back up his claim of self-defense.

While his wife, Phyllis, isn't happy to learn about what he's been up to, Lou hopes that reading his work will secure her support, only to be stunned when she tells him just how bad his poetry really is. After finding the cash in Damian's room, Sheila worries that her son is dealing drugs. So, after agreeing to speak with Damian in order to keep Sheila from learning the truth, Tommy tries to give up drinking in order to regain control of his life. And already upset that Janet doesn't share his anger over Colleen's new tattoo, Tommy is further dismayed when he's asked to repair a clogged sink before his wife's new boyfriend arrives for dinner.

As Tommy returns home to find Colleen's boyfriend trying to sneak out of his house, Roger decides that his relationship with Janet isn't working out. And after Janet says that she can't live in the neighborhood any longer, Tommy finds evidence that she is looking for a house in Kansas. On the night of the big hockey game, Tommy's rage boils over as he takes it out on Ryan, while at the gay bar, Jerry sees little chance of finding a sympathetic witness. Finally, as Tommy cannot keep from drinking, Jerry shows up looking for someone to talk to, while in Boston, the beleaguered captain's gay son, Peter, learns about his legal problems.

Directed by: John Fortenberry

Written by: Denis Leary & Peter Tolan

3: DNA

As Tommy struggles to remember the name of someone he's been sleeping with, and Jerry balks at accepting a suspension for attacking a gay ex-fireman, a woman who's looking for Franco approaches Sean. Explaining that Nez is a violent alcoholic and drug abuser, Franco asks Sean to send her packing. But after seeing through their ruse and then luring Sean into a date, Nez corners Franco at work to tell him he is the father of her five-year-old daughter. Meanwhile, as Tommy and Janet square off over Colleen's attending a concert with her boyfriend, Mike balks at the apparent sexual interest of Andrew, the man whose life he saved.

Over dinner, Tommy listens to Sheila worry that her son, Damian, must be dealing drugs. Though he phones Damian with a threat to cut off his payments for harassing Janet's boyfriend, Tommy is intrigued when his nephew offers to have Roger's car repossessed. And after learning that the woman he thought Sheila was involved with was only her psychic, their date suddenly turns amorous and forces Tommy into an uncomfortable encounter with his late cousin's ghost. Meanwhile, after Mike claims that he isn't gay, he discovers that Andrew and his beautiful fiancée want to thank him by having a ménage à trois. And after a DNA test proving Franco's paternity has Nez threatening to sue, Jerry is suspended pending the outcome of his hearing.

At the scene of a car accident, Tommy identifies one of the injured drivers as Colleen's boyfriend, and then realizes that his daughter has been seriously injured in the crash as well. Hurrying to the hospital, he angrily sends Roger packing before settling in with Janet for a long and uncomfortable wait. And when he runs into his cousin, Father Mickey Gavin, at the hospital chapel, Tommy inconsolably laments how much he would like to turn back the clock and start life anew.

Directed by: Jace Alexander

Written by: Peter Tolan & Denis Leary and John Scurti

Music: "Summer's Over" by The Stratford 4,
"Said And Done" by Tyrone Wells

4: ORPHANS

As Tommy tries to insure that Colleen won't want to see her boyfriend anymore, and Jerry realizes just how serious the department is about his suspension, Franco lam-bastes Sean about his dating Nez. But, following a violent encounter with another woman that leaves Nez dead and her daughter, Keela, in the care of her drug-addicted roommate, Sean presses Franco to take responsibility for the girl. And while balking at first, seeing the squalid conditions she's living in is all it takes to convince Franco to take her home. Meanwhile, a fight breaks out when Roger asks that Tommy stop coming between him and Janet. And, already unhappy that his union lawyer is homosexual, Jerry's case may have to rely on the testimony of his gay son, Peter.

Following a showdown over breakfast that convinces him to place Keela in foster care, Franco and Sean come to blows. After claiming he talked to a dead girl trapped by an apartment building collapse, Tommy finds his dad and a pair of prostitutes at his Uncle Teddy's house. Nevertheless, while pressing him to go home, Tommy learns just how unhappy and sexually unsatisfied his dad has been during his forty-seven years of marriage. So, in the wake of the news about his dad, and following encounters with the ghosts of his cousin and the dead girl, Tommy decides to let Janet get on with her life, even if it means her and the kids moving away.

At his departmental hearing, news that the bartender will testify has Jerry hoping that he won't have to rely on Peter. However, when the bartender claims that Jerry provoked the confrontation with his anti-gay remarks, Peter steps in to get his father off the hook by claiming that he's always accepted his homosexual lifestyle. Finally, as a relieved Jerry quickly reverts to his old ways by turning his back on his son, and Franco and Sean try to patch things up between them, Tommy is jumped, and badly beaten, by Roger's friends.

Directed by: Jace Alexander

Written by: Salvatore Stabile

Music: "Chasing Dreams" by Magnet

5: REVENGE

While plotting to get revenge for the beating he received from Roger's friends, Tommy tricks Sean into making a date with a beautiful woman who is really a transvestite. Much to Tommy's delight, Sean responds by betting that he can get her in bed by the end of the week. And as psychologist Dr. Thompkins presses Lou to read his poetry, Franco asks Tommy for help finding the foster home of his daughter, Keela. Meanwhile, with Johnny's help, Tommy has Roger arrested at Janet's house. And while Janet doubts that Roger could be responsible for the assault, Johnny convinces her that he's about to confess.

Pressed to admit that he's interested in something more than just the easy sex, Tommy gives Lauren a less-than-heartfelt gift to honor the anniversary of the day they met. After Lauren asks to be invited over, Tommy comes home to find her waiting for him and reluctantly agrees to let her stay. But when Janet shows up to discuss reconciling their broken marriage, Tommy is in deep trouble after a showdown between the two women reveals that he doesn't even know Lauren's name. Meanwhile, as Franco kidnaps Keela from her abusive foster father, Lou is stunned to learn that none of the members of Dr. Thompkins's 9/11 survivors support group were even at the World Trade Center.

Telling Jerry that he knows the truth about the "woman" he's been dating, Sean says that he's now going to turn the tables on Tommy by telling him that they are getting married. As Franco seeks help in avoiding an arrest for kidnapping Keela, once Johnny assures him that foster parents will never complain as long as they continue receiving their check from the state, he stashes the little girl at his mother's house for now. Finally, after his house is firebombed, Tommy learns that it was Lauren who started the blaze.

Directed by: Adam Berstein

Written by: Michael Caleo

6: BUTTERFLY

As Franco talks Sean into auditioning for the annual firefighter calendar, Jerry sends Tommy to see a department psychiatrist about his talking to dead people. Spotted at headquarters by someone he knows, Tommy claims he's only submitting the paperwork to have a park jogging path named after their late colleague, Vito Costello. But instead of giving him some time off, the doctor prescribes anti-depressants, sleeping pills, and Viagra. After an angry showdown, Tommy is caught eavesdropping on Janet and Roger by their neighbor, psychotherapist Robert Shinsky. When asked about the medication, Shinsky recommends it only as a last resort. So, after learning that his neighbor wants to put a new deck on his house, Tommy offers to do the job.

As his crew is working on the deck, Tommy asks Shinsky for advice about Janet. Already unhappy with Tommy's badgering, Shinsky is even more upset when his friends want to talk, too. But when Janet shows up drunk at his house later that night, Tommy ducks out to call Shinsky before agreeing to go to bed with her. Meanwhile, as Sean is chosen for the calendar, Andrew tells Mike how much it upset his fiancée, Geneva, to have him walk out on their offer of a ménage à trois. But after agreeing to apologize, Mike thinks he's going to bed with Geneva alone, only to find he's been lured into having sex with the couple after all.

After calling to tell his dad about reconciling with Janet, his brother, Johnny, drops by to complain about not being told, too. But Tommy is soon thrown for a loop when Janet tells him that they can never get back together. And after telling Janet that she needs to see a psychiatrist, he tracks down Shinsky to complain about his advice. Finally, after Andrew attacks Mike for thinking he could sleep with Geneva without his permission, Tommy seeks comfort in a bottle before attending the dedication of Vito's park path.

Directed by: Adam Berstein

Written by: Robert Krausz

Music: "Karaoke Soul" by Tom McRae

7: INCHES

As Tommy struggles with his recurring nightmares of 9/11, the crew is embroiled in a heated debate over how best to measure their sexual equipment. Once Jerry establishes a definitive standard, only Billy balks at a contest to identify the house's best endowed fireman. Already thrown for a loop after his dad called for help after Uncle Teddy came home with a monkey, Tommy discovers that he is now the caretaker of Katy's new dog. Already arguing about who's responsible for the messy pet, Tommy and Janet square off over Colleen's suspension for kissing a girl at school. And as Tommy finds comfort in the fact that Colleen is having a relationship with a girl, Mike is surprised when his girlfriend's daughter, Nicole, comes to stay for a week.

Told that her son is dealing drugs, upon arriving to escort Sheila to a party for Bobby Vincent's widow, Tommy confiscates Damien's stash, but only after making sure he knows which pills can be used to calm down both Uncle Teddy and his crazed monkey. Uncomfortable with all the attention he is getting at the party from a widow named Gloria, Tommy soon realizes that, because he's Sheila's escort, the other widows have started to eye him as being available for sex. Meanwhile, as Tommy's dad worries that he may have given Uncle Teddy a drug overdose, and Mike doesn't know what to do when Nicole makes a pass at him, a girlfriend's effort to help Franco win the contest forces them to call Lou for help. And after he can't stop seeing the fire victims that have been haunting him, Tommy seeks refuge in his cousin, Mickey's, church.

After fielding an angry call from Sheila, Tommy arrives with his crew at a deserted warehouse whose homeless residents have been overcome by a fire's smoke and heat where, after rescuing two teenaged girls, he watches in horror as the floor collapses, sending Billy to his death. At Billy's funeral, Tommy learns that Gloria has been telling everyone that they are having sex. But after convincing Sheila that the claims are false, Tommy finds that his sexually ferocious response to her advances drives out his visions of her late husband, Jimmy. Finally, though the initial results point to Franco, word of Billy's size makes him the contest's posthumous winner.

Directed by: John Fortenberry

Written by: Denis Leary

Music: "All I Can Do" by Tyrone Wells

8: ALARM

In the wake of Billy Warren's death, NYPD Detective Timo Gavin reluctantly fuels his brother, Tommy's, quest for vengeance by pointing him to the homeless teens who were saved from the blaze. And after one of them admits that the fire started when she was forced to fend off some unwanted sexual advances, they tell Tommy where the homeless crack addict is staying. Meanwhile, as a bad tip causes Jerry to lose big on a baseball bet, the firefighters learn that a woman is being sent to replace Billy. And as he and Janet continue to disagree over their daughter's lesbian romance, after finally admitting that he feels better about Colleen having sex with girls instead of boys, Tommy encourages her to invite Jennifer over to his house.

While Lou is surprised at Billy's ex-wife, Sondra's, sudden interest in his poetry, a discarded pregnancy test found at Janet's house sparks a confrontation between Tommy and Colleen that, even though she isn't pregnant, causes problems with Jennifer. Told that he must settle up his gambling losses by the end of the week, Jerry is furious to learn that his wife, Jeannie, accidentally threw out his hidden cash. So, with Jerry forced to scrounge around for $5,000 to keep his bookie off his back, despite being uncomfortable with the interest that Paula's daughter has shown in him, Mike is lured into having sex with her. Meanwhile, as Lou digs in to resist taking on a female firefighter, helping an elderly woman escape a dangerous gas leak allows Jerry to surreptitiously pocket her diamond ring and hidden money.

As Lou tries keeping Sondra at bay, a showdown over the pregnancy test has Tommy thinking that a baby might help patch up his broken marriage. Then, with Sean and Franco along to help, he tracks down and nearly kills the drug addict he holds responsible for Billy's death. Finally, once Paula sends Mike packing after learning of his affair with Nicole, after giving in to Sondra, Lou isn't sure what to do next. And as Jerry guiltily returns the stolen ring and money, news that the pregnancy test was mistaken forces Janet to admit that even a new baby could never reunite her and Tommy. So, after Tommy uses sex with Sheila to ease his pain, Jerry and Lou are disappointed when no one wants to help freeze out the new female firefighter after all.

Directed by: John Fortenberry

Written by: Salvatore Stabile

Music: "I'll Be Your Man" by The Black Keys

9: IMMORTAL

Now that he's having sex with Sheila, Tommy cannot shake his visions of her late husband's ghost. On top of dreaming about Jimmy, the shaky finances that have him owing Janet four thousand dollars have also led to some angry and reckless driving that gets him cited by a vengeful cop. At work, female firefighter Laura Miles has made it clear that Jerry is in no position to deny her request for a private bathroom. And as Tommy offers to help reunite Colleen and her girlfriend, Jennifer, Andrew apologizes for the beating he gave Mike following their failed three-way with his fiancée, and then insists that he move in with him now that Geneva has left.

While an encounter with the new firefighter convinces him that she's interested in something more than a professional relationship, before Tommy can act, a fire provides Laura with her first test—one that she fails after trying to keep Tommy from risking his own life to save a young girl, and then becoming overcome by smoke as she and Franco are inside the burning building. And while Laura insists that it will never happen again, Jerry warns her that she won't have many more chances. Meanwhile, as Tommy intervenes on his daughter's behalf with Jennifer, he hopes to avoid another encounter with Jimmy by asking his brother, Timo, to arrange for a hotel room where he and Sheila can meet. However, after their sexual escapade, Tommy is unnerved when Sheila suspects that he's seen her late husband's ghost.

Once Mike settles in for a drunken night at his new apartment, Andrew's alcohol- and drug-fueled efforts to force him into bed are met with a baseball bat to the head. Seeking refuge with Tommy after losing his house in Atlantic City, Uncle Teddy attempts suicide. But after failing leaves him feeling invincible, Teddy parlays his remaining cash into a bundle at the racetrack, leaving Tommy with the money he needs to pay Janet. Finally, Laura gets a chance to redeem herself when the crew is sent to stop two gay men who are having sex high in a tree.

Directed by: Jace Alexander

Written by: Dennis Leary & Peter Tolan

10: MOM

Pressured by his mom into dating a friend's daughter, Mike is disappointed—but not surprised—to find that she's overweight. But after forcing him to admit to his ambivalence about their date, Theresa proceeds to give Mike the best sex he's ever had. After insisting that Jerry keep her new bathroom private, Laura watches Tommy defy orders to rescue a dog and wonders how long it will be before his recklessness gets him... or someone else... killed. Meanwhile, as Sean frets over how the new firefighter's calendar makes him seem gay, Lou tells his wife, Phyllis, about his affair with Sondra, only to learn she is seeing another fireman.

As things with Shelia look to be headed for rocky

ground, Tommy returns home where, after learning that Uncle Teddy has invited his racetrack tipster, Arlo, to stay for a few days, Janet arrives to tell him that, while he was out, his mother died. As the death sends his dad into an emotional tailspin, at the wake, Tommy learns that, with Timo leaving town on vacation and Johnny moving to Philadelphia, he's the one who will have to be responsible for their father. And when Tommy coolly rebuffs Sheila's attempt at comforting him, he must then convince Mickey, Johnny, and Janet that there's nothing going on between them. Meanwhile, when he won't take her to the wake, Theresa suspects that Mike is embarrassed by her weight.

At a calendar autograph session, Sean learns why he's become an object of attention for so many gay men. And after Lou tracks him down at work, Phyllis's boyfriend, Greg Kelly, reveals that sex isn't a big part of their relationship. Called to his parents' home to find his dad collapsed after smoking too much marijuana, Tommy insists that he come and live with him. But when they arrive at home, Tommy is shocked to discover that Uncle Teddy has accidentally killed the dog he has grown to love. Finally, after learning that Jerry has been secretly using her private bathroom, Laura lays a trap that will make sure he'll never do it again.

Directed by: Jace Alexander

Written by: Peter Tolan & Denis Leary

11: LEAVING

Already being hounded by Janet for money to replace her air conditioner, Tommy gets a stern warning from Jerry to steer clear of Sheila. And as Jerry complains about a bookie who's forgotten to pay off a big bet, and Franco returns to work with his daughter, Keela, in tow, a trio of rowdy firefighters from Massachusetts ask to stay at the firehouse while they construct a 9/11 memorial. Asking them to keep a low profile, Sean leaves them at the station while he's at a fire where he apologizes to Laura for all the harassment. Meanwhile, after an uncomfortable phone call from Sheila, Tommy learns that Janet is lying about the air conditioner. And when Mike suggests that they consider living together, he's surprised to learn that Theresa is bulimic.

Ordered to get his daughter out of the firehouse, when Franco asks his girlfriend, China, for help, she balks, telling him that he'll have to choose between her and Keela. Though surprised when he is paid off for a bet he never made, Jerry has second thoughts about returning it when he learns that his longtime bookie has Alzheimer's. After his dinner invitation to Laura is rebuffed, Sean is startled when he spots Mike and the overweight Theresa. And after Laura complains about how everyone is talking about Theresa behind Mike's back, Sean raises suspicions when he asks that Lou stop harassing the new female firefighter. Meanwhile, when confronted about her lies, Janet tells Tommy that she needs the money for household expenses.

As Tommy's recklessness continues to call his judgment into question, the memorial built by Sean's friends sets the firehouse ablaze. While a visit to the firehouse that ignites rumors about an affair forces Tommy to order Sheila to leave and promise to see her later, Sean is delighted when Laura asks him to dinner. Then, as a misunderstanding accidentally reveals that Laura and Sean are sexually involved, a call for help from another firehouse leads Jerry to realize that his wife is starting to exhibit symptoms of Alzheimer's. And after Arlo comes through with the money for Janet, Tommy learns that his dad has left for Ireland. Finally, as Theresa and Mike's relationship starts to crumble, China makes good on her threat to walk out on Franco. And as Janet stashes the money with the rest of the cash she's hoarding, Tommy arrives for his showdown with Sheila.

Directed by: Peter Tolan

Written by: Denis Leary & Peter Tolan

Music: "Just A Dream" by Griffin House

12: SANCTUARY

To make the next hockey game with the NYPD a wild affair, Tommy mends fences with his ex-co-captain, Ryan, who offers to enlist a fireman who is on leave for beating up three cops. As Lou's affair with Sondra heats up, and Mike comes to grips with Theresa's eating disorder, Franco counsels Sean on how to dump Carol, a woman he says is a bad kisser. And after another day at the track with Uncle Teddy and Arlo leaves him with plenty of cash for Janet and Sheila, Tommy is startled when Laura questions his motives and his sanity. Then, after she's the only one who can stop an angry man from attacking the firefighters removing his

morbidly obese mother's corpse from her apartment, Laura gains some credibility with the crew.

Tommy's plans for the hockey game play out perfectly when the police team loses their cool. Then, once the firefighters' win is assured, they unleash a cascade of violence that sends both teams tumbling into the street. When claiming to be gay can't help Sean get rid of Carol, Lou gladly agrees when his wife's boyfriend tells him that Phyllis wants a divorce. And after a bad day at the track forces Arlo to admit that his luck has run out, he stuns Teddy by claiming that he's in love with him. Meanwhile, during a visit to the firehouse, Father Mickey Gavin confirms that his cousin is having an affair with Sheila. So, when confronted by his colleagues, who give him a vicious beating for the indiscretion, Tommy blurts out that Sheila is pregnant.

After learning that Mickey revealed his secret, a call sends the crew to a fire where, as he is searching the building with Laura, Tommy becomes disoriented by his ghostly visions. But when Laura calls for help, Franco arrives and is injured when the ceiling collapses. As the tragedy causes both Jerry and Perroli to warn him to clean up his act, Tommy asks for a transfer and, after punishing Mickey, heads home to find that Janet has moved after learning about Sheila. Finally, as Franco's accident leaves Mike turning to Theresa for comfort, Jerry learns that wife, Jeannine, has Alzheimer's.

Directed by: Jace Alexander

Written by: Peter Tolan & Denis Leary

Music: "Fell On Bad Days" by Rubyhorse

1: VOICEMAIL

Fighting nightmares about Franco's injury, Janet's selling the house and leaving with their kids, Sheila's pregnancy, and even premonitions of his own death, New York City firefighter Tommy Gavin is now living alone in an illegal East Village sublet after being transferred to Staten Island. Far from the action at his old Manhattan firehouse, 62 Truck, Tommy realizes that he is going to have to get his life back on track and calls Father Mickey to ask about returning to an AA meeting. With his parking tickets piling up, he then turns to his brother, Johnny, for help getting them dismissed before asking him and their lawyer-cousin, Eddie, to find Janet. But Johnny finally has enough of his out-of-control behavior and takes his brother to task after he's arrested for a drunken attack on some street vendors working at Ground Zero.

Now that Lou finds being divorced and available has made him unattractive to his girlfriend, and Jerry struggles to cope with his wife's Alzheimer's, Sean is goaded into secretly taking a pornographic picture with Laura's camera. But after innocently trying to get the pictures developed nearly gets her arrested, Laura turns the tables and exacts revenge on Sean. As Franco nurses the wounds he sustained while rescuing Tommy, and Mike discovers that incompatibility has doomed his relationship with Teresa, the one person still willing to stand by Tommy's side—Sheila—catches him drinking and bolts.

While doing his best to try and cover it up, Tommy cannot disguise his unhappiness with his Staten Island assignment and tells Lou that he would love nothing more than to be back at 62 Truck. Although Lou wants to help, he insists that Tommy give up drinking and call to square things with Franco. So, after calling to arrange to meet Mickey at an AA meeting, Tommy places a call to Franco, only to have him refuse to talk. As a result, after a difficult phone call with his kids, a drunken Tommy comes within inches of killing himself before finally showing up at the AA meeting with Mickey.

Directed by: Jace Alexander

Written by: Denis Leary & Peter Tolan

Music: "Burn" by Ray LaMontagne

2: HARMONY

As Lou and Jerry find Chief Perroli vehemently opposed to bringing him back to 62 Truck, Tommy is hunkered down in his new Staten Island assignment waiting for some good news. When asked by his new colleagues to join their barbershop quartet for a national competition in Ohio, Tom-my can barley disguise his contempt. Yet, after a phone call from Colleen reveals that she and the rest of the family are hiding out near Columbus, Tommy joins the quartet in hopes of being able to see them. As Tommy looks to curry Sheila's favor by telling her that he's stopped drinking, Uncle Teddy's gambling lands him in trouble with the mob. And after he's unable to convince Teresa to take him back, an angry and hurt Mike starts to stalk her and her new boyfriend.

Soon after arriving in Ohio for the competition, Tommy borrows the SUV belonging to another one of the firefighters and heads off to track down Janet. Finding her dating a local firefighter, he insists that they are still legally married and demands that she and their kids return with him to New York or face kidnapping charges. However, when he gives her a few minutes to get their things together, Janet sneaks away with the children. Meanwhile, with Jerry doing everything he can to deal with his wife's Alzheimer's, and Franco developing an unhealthy reliance on his prescription painkillers, even though Sean convinces him to start dating again, Mike finds that he misses Teresa too much.

Upon finding that Janet has given him the slip, Tommy ends up getting the worst end of an encounter with her boyfriend, Steve. Beaten and bloodied, he makes a futile attempt to find his family before going to a bar where, after resisting the temptation to take a drink, he makes his way back to the barbershop quartet contest to join his co-workers for the long drive back home. Finally, as Lou's efforts to blackmail Perroli into reinstating Tommy backfire, Mike sullenly looks for a way to get Teresa back.

Directed by: Jace Alexander

Written by: Peter Tolan & Denis Leary

Music: "Trouble" by Ray LaMontagne

3: BALLS (A.K.A. HOME)

As Tommy fights back some disturbing visions of Jesus, problems with his illegal sublet, and Sheila's roiling emotions, Lou and Jerry try to convince Chief Perrolli to take him back—an especially difficult task now that the crew has grown fond of the courageous and multi-talented Sully, not to mention Franco's steadfast refusal to forgive him for causing his injuries. However, even when Perrolli offers to relent if the crew unanimously agrees, a vote reveals that

Franco isn't the only obstacle in Tommy's way. Meanwhile, after he's told that Uncle Teddy has most likely been killed over his gambling debts, Tommy learns that his father is living in a fancy Park Avenue apartment. And though Tommy disapproves of his marriage to a wealthy Korean widow, his dad refuses to consider giving up his new arrangement.

Taking Sully's advice, Mike sets out to win Teresa back, only to have the plan backfire when she gets a restraining order after he takes a swing at her new boyfriend. Needing time to date the nurse who is giving him a steady supply of powerful prescription painkillers, Franco asks Laura to baby-sit his daughter, Keela. Begging off at first, she agrees to help when Franco offers to pick up her bar tab for a night out with her friends. But after showing up back at his house after a few drinks, she makes it clear that she wants to take him to bed.

After giving in to pressure from Lou, Franco's reunion with Tommy is interrupted when the crew of 62 Truck is called to fight a fire at an underground gay sex club. But, horrified to discover that a man they found chained to a wall of the club dressed in women's clothes is none other than Sully, when asked to vote again, they unanimously agree to let Tommy return. Finally, as Mike obtains a gun to use in his effort to get Teresa back, Sheila keeps news of her miscarriage a secret from Tommy and her son, Damien.

Directed by: John Fortenberry
Written by: Denis Leary & Peter Tolan
Music: "The Widow" by The Mars Volta

4: TWAT

Still unable to shake the unsettling visions that he's been having since he stopped drinking, Tommy's anger over having his truck towed causes him to attack the beat cop he holds responsible. Though he gets the best of the officer in their brief fight, Tommy comes away the worse for wear when he breaks his hand. Then, after letting everyone at his AA meeting know just what he thinks of them and their problems, he heads for a rendezvous with Sheila. But when he has trouble performing and Sheila insists that he take a drink to get over it, Tommy leaves instead.

While spending the night together has Franco and Laura wondering about what comes next, Tommy's dad finds that, instead of being murdered over some unpaid gambling debts, Uncle Teddy is making big money working as a plus-size catalog model. As Sean offers to take Mike to an informal shooting range to blow off some steam over his being dumped by Teresa, Tommy becomes a hero on his first day back at work with his daring rescue of a little girl and her cat. And after Laura formally complains about a derogatory slur hurled at her by Lou, listening to Tommy and the others defend their verbal assaults on one another as a form of camaraderie causes her to question her reaction.

As Franco works to keep up his steady supply of painkillers by continuing to date a nurse, the trip to the firing range with Sean goes awry when Mike accidentally shoots a cat. And though the tall and attractive vet they seek out for help is unable to save the mortally wounded animal, she makes sure that Mike doesn't leave without her phone number. Finally, after another round of disturbing hallucinations makes his struggle to stay sober even more difficult, Tommy is stunned when his daughter, Colleen, shows up at the firehouse.

Directed by: John Fortenberry
Written by: Peter Tolan & Denis Leary
Music: "Rebirth Of The Cool" by The Afghan Whigs

5: SENSITIVITY

With Perrolli asking to Mickey to help make sure his brother keeps his nose clean, all-too-aware of what getting caught will mean for his future, Tommy does everything he can to hide his drug and alcohol use from the chief. And now that Colleen has run away from home to live with him, Tommy is determined to do whatever it takes—even kidnapping—to get his other two kids away from Janet. Meanwhile, as Franco tries to keep Laura from learning that he's dating a nurse who's giving him painkillers, Mike fails to adequately explain what it is he likes about large women.

As their dad presses Uncle Teddy to get work as a model, too, Tommy and Johnny are startled to learn that, as a result of an affair that lasted more than thirty years, they have a brother and sister they never knew about. With the truth about their dad's secret family shedding some light on their upbringing, Johnny warns Tommy against doing anything illegal to get his children back. So, to continue keeping Perrolli in the dark about his drug and alcohol problem, Tommy goes to as many A.A. meetings as he can manage. Meanwhile, as Tommy's dad gets some disappointing news about his prospects for a modeling career, when Jerry arrives home to find his Alzheimer's-suffering wife, Jeannie, in bed with a stranger, he calls his estranged gay son, Peter, for help.

As a result of Laura's sexual harassment complaint against Lou, the entire crew of 62 Truck is ordered to attend a sensitivity training where Tommy and his fellow firefighters are nearly thrown out after voicing their contempt for the class. Once Lou makes it painfully clear that, unlike her, he has few options other than being a firefighter, Laura takes his confession as an apology for his crass behavior. And in the wake of another hallucination about Mary Magdalene and Jesus Christ, Tommy tries to patch things up with a romantic evening with Sheila, only to find evidence that she's no longer pregnant.

Directed by: Peter Tolan

Written by: Denis Leary & Peter Tolan

Music: "I Want You" by Cobra Verde,
"Hallelujah" by Ryan Adams

6: REUNION

Already suspicious that Sheila may not be pregnant, Tommy solicits some advice from Laura before setting out to find proof. Continuing to ignore his brother Johnny's warnings, he pushes ahead with his plan to kidnap his other two children. However, Tommy's plans are dashed when the FBI agent who is his sublet apartment's legal tenant orders him to move out because of the neighbors' complaints. Meanwhile Sean's colleagues warn him against dating a woman who is sleeping her way through the entire fire department. And as Jerry struggles to find a way to talk to his gay son, Peter, Lou attends a reception for bone marrow donors and survivors, only to find that Leon, the man whose life he saved, isn't especially grateful.

After learning his name, Tommy calls on Sheila's obstetrician, who reveals the truth about the miscarriage. But before he can leave, Tommy is confronted by the ghost of his cousin—Sheila's late husband, Jimmy—who dishes out a brutal beating as he insists that he do whatever it takes to get her pregnant again. Ignoring the demand, Tommy heads for Sheila's house instead and, with a frightened Colleen looking on, he angrily confronts Sheila with the truth. Meanwhile, as Lou decides to let Leon know how he feels

about being snubbed, Jerry learns that Sean's new girlfriend, Heather, is a firebug. So, as Sean dumps Heather after confronting her about the fires she's started, Jerry finds the courage to ask Peter about what it's like to be gay.

When he can't find his pain medication, Franco takes it out on his daughter, Keela, unaware that Tommy has been stealing his pills. However, the drug-addicted firefighter's rage turns to fear after he discovers Keela unconscious from an accidental overdose. Accused of being ungrateful for the bone marrow donation, Leon offers to make things right by taking Lou out for a drink. But when he then tries sticking Lou with the tab, things sour between them. Finally, with Colleen's help, Tommy kidnaps Katy and Conor from their school. But before long, they have him questioning whether he's made a mistake. And when the firefighters answer a call at her apartment, Sean is stunned to find that, as a result of their breakup, Heather committed suicide.

Directed by: Peter Tolan

Written by: Peter Tolan & Denis Leary

Music: "Broken" by Alaska!

7: SHAME

Having stashed his kids with his dad, Tommy joins Lou in secretly taking up residence at the firehouse. Although he and Tommy can't find new places to live, Lou does run into Sondra, the woman who dumped him after he left his wife for her. Knowing that she's attracted to men who are already attached, Lou tells Sondra that he's dating someone and then, taking Tommy's advice, hires a prostitute to help convince her that it's true. And while the atmosphere at his dad's apartment is tense, Tommy can only think to ask Uncle Teddy for a connection to supply him with painkillers. Meanwhile, Jerry's tolerance is tested when his son's boyfriend, Steven, arrives for a visit. And when Franco brings Keela home from the hospital following her overdose, Laura stays to help.

After rescuing a severely burned young boy from an apartment fire, Tommy agrees to take Franco along to a drug rehab meeting, but only after pressing him for any painkillers he may have stashed somewhere. After a heated argument with Sheila reveals that she is now seeing a woman, Tommy is at the hospital consoling the mother of the injured boy when he slips into another hallucination, telling Jesus that he will only consider believing in God if the youngster recovers. Meanwhile, despite his recent run of bad luck, Lou encourages Sean not to give up on dating.

As Tommy, Mickey, and Johnny attend a church picnic being given by their recently discovered half-brother, Father Murphy, Sean accompanies Franco to his rehab in hopes of meeting some women. Though Franco hesitates to openly discuss his drug problem, Sean wastes no time in introducing himself as a former crack user to Molly, one of the recovering addicts. While doing everything he can think of to contact the dealer recommended by Uncle Teddy, Tommy finds that caring for his kids is already trying his patience. And when Mickey suggests that a young boy that Father Murphy has been caring for is actually his son, Tommy doesn't want to believe it. Finally, as Jerry loses his composure after walking in on Peter and Steven having sex, Franco admits that even Keela's brush with death hasn't been enough to break him of his addiction.

Directed by: Jace Alexander

Written by: Evan Reilly

Music: "My Old Man" by The Walkmen

8: BELIEVE

While trying to keep his relationship with Shelia from engulfing his life, Tommy gains an edge in his competition with Johnny for their half-sister, Mariel's, attention. Although Mariel is eager to have sex, even the suggestion that they might not have the same father can't overcome Tommy's reservations. After criticizing Mickey for suspecting that their half-brother, Father Murphy, is a child molester, Tommy is at the hospital with the boy he saved when, during another hallucination, he's encouraged to pray for the restoration of his marriage to Janet. Meanwhile, as Franco asks Laura to move in with him, and Jerry learns that his wife and son are planning a birthday party for Peter's boyfriend, Steven, Lou's ruse to keep Sondra interested in sex gets harder to maintain when he becomes interested in Candy—the prostitute he's hired to help with the deception.

Though everyone but Laura balked at the invitation, even after Jerry orders them to attend Steven's party, Tommy and company refuse to mingle with the decidedly gay crowd. However, after Laura insists that she and Franco join in the fun, and

then Mike and Sean are unable to resist, too, only Tommy and Lou are left outside. But as Lou gears up the deception when Sondra calls demanding to know where he is, Franco and Laura's plans to live together are derailed when Sean unwittingly tells her about the nurse Franco was dating to feed his drug addiction. Meanwhile, things come unglued at the elder Gavin's apartment when Janet arrives to see her kids.

As Franco begs Laura not to leave him, and Sean and Mike pretend to be gay in order to impress two women at the party, a call from Uncle Teddy sends Tommy rushing to his dad's apartment. Now on his own, Lou calls on Candy to help him keep up appearances for Sondra. However, deciding that he can't keep it up any longer, he tells Sondra the truth so he can spend the evening with Candy. Finally, as Jerry's frustration with Peter's homosexuality wanes, and a suspicious Mickey stalks Father Murphy, Tommy's prayers are answered when Janet decides she wants to give their marriage a second chance and the badly burned boy awakes from his coma.

Directed by: Jace Alexander

Written by: Evan Reilly

Music: "I Shall Believe" by Sheryl Crow

9: REBIRTH

Although he and Janet have agreed to try and reconcile their differences, Tommy is still surprised at her sexually playful attitude. So, after Lou suggests that Janet may be on antidepressants, Tommy sneaks a look inside her purse during a family dinner at his dad's apartment and finds the pills that are responsible for her improved attitude. Although he wants to undo the damage his loose talk has caused, Sean's efforts to patch things up between Laura and Franco only make matters worse. So, desperate to regain Laura's trust, Franco asks Lou to help him out by writing a poem. Meanwhile, in the wake of Steven Reilly's birthday party, the suspicion at 62 Truck is that Mike is gay. And after Lou defends her when she's accosted on the street by a former customer, Candy invites him up to her apartment, only to have him balk at staying overnight.

As the police start turning up the heat in advance of their annual hockey game against the fire department, Tommy learns that Janet has started looking for an apartment where they live can together as a family again. However, when Tommy looks to get some of the same medication Janet is taking, his doctor refuses to help him out. As Mike admits that he has started hanging around gay men as a way to meet women, Tommy fails miserably to use the church confessional to repent, so he turns his energies towards trying to make things right by helping out at the firehouse.

After it's found that the poems to Laura that Franco thought were written by Lou were actually Tommy's work, everyone is stunned. When this new and improved Tommy Gavin miraculously survives a fall during a fire at an abandoned warehouse, Franco asks him to write another poem for Laura when Lou's efforts fall short. And when pressed by Lou about what's going on, Tommy admits that the drugs he's been stealing from Janet have transformed him into a new man. However, his teammates are less than pleased when, during their game against the cops, the medication dilutes Tommy's killer instinct.

Directed by: Jefery Levy

Written by: Denis Leary & Peter Tolan

Music: "Pussywillow" by Greg Dulli

10: BRAINS

When his son returns home to Boston, Jerry looks for help to care for his ailing wife. As Lou offers to help Candy quit working as a prostitute, Tommy continues stealing Janet's anti-depressants, while encouraging her to get the prescription refilled as soon as possible. And when the brother of the boy that Father Murphy is suspected of molesting claims to have been his victim, too, Tommy reluctantly admits that Mickey was right about their half-brother.

After a poem copied from a schoolbook makes Laura more suspicious than ever, Lou denies being the author, only to then turn around and implicate Tommy. Already upset by his alleged half-sister, Mariel's, efforts to get him into bed, Tommy is forced to respond when Sheila accuses her new girlfriend of abuse. Meanwhile, as Sean introduces Jerry to a stripper who can help him find a nurse for Jeannie, and Tommy admits to writing the poems, a distraught Kevin Lopez produces a letter that proves Father Murphy's guilt.

As Jerry starts interviewing nurses, Tommy's tries confronting Debbie about Sheila's accusations, only to end up giving her sexual advice instead. Finally, even when he's shown Kevin's letter, Father Murphy insists that it doesn't prove anything. However, after admitting that he was also abused as a boy, the pedophile priest is arrested after he and the Gavin brothers helplessly witness Kevin's suicide.

Directed by: Jefery Levy

Written by: Mike Martineau

Music: "Run" by Snow Patrol

11: BITCH

As he relies on his wife's anti-depressants to fight the visions of his late cousin, Jimmy, a frantic call from Sheila brings Tommy to counsel her son, Damien, after he announces that he is following family tradition by joining the fire department. Taking Connor along, Tommy does his best to dissuade Damien. But when he can't bring himself to talk him out of it, Tommy gives Damien his late father's badge and offers to explain everything to his mom. Yet, listening from outside the door, Connor overhears Tommy and Damien talking about his affair with Sheila. Meanwhile, after he and Laura agree to take a break from each other, Franco warns Tommy to steer clear. And when Laura starts dating another firefighter, Sean urges Franco to get even by dating a porn star.

After hiring his new neighbor, Rose, to help care for his ailing wife, Jerry is embarrassed over an incident when she brings Jeannie to the firehouse. And after being invited up to her apartment, Lou is disappointed when a call from a client forces Candy to cut their evening short. Meanwhile, after Laura accuses him of being interested in her, Tommy denies it as he gives her advice on how to deal with Franco. And upon returning from Atlantic City to find that his wealthy wife has died, Tommy's dad realizes that he's now rich.

Following a romantic dinner with Janet, Tommy is preparing for bed when Mike calls to tell him that the hockey team has decided he isn't aggressive enough to be their coach any more. So, concluding that it is the only way to regain his credibility, Tommy stops taking Janet's anti-depressants—a decision that gives him back his edge, but confuses his family. Finally, when pressed, Candy tells Lou that her pimp has agreed to let her quit—for $30,000. And as Franco's efforts to make Laura jealous backfire, Tommy resorts to violence on the ice in order to prove that he is still capable of being the hockey team's coach.

Directed by: John Fortenberry
Written by: John Scurti
Music: "Make It Up" by Ben Kweller

12: HAPPY

As they begin to realize that Mrs. Ng's death is going to make their father very wealthy, the Gavin family begins looking forward to a not-too-distant future where they will all be well off. As Janet solicits his reluctant participation in a ceremony to renew their wedding vows, Tommy decides to share his newfound fortune with his friends at work. However, as they are discussing how to redecorate their Park Avenue apartment, the Gavins are all surprised by the appearance of the family's estranged black sheep daughter, Maggie. And though their father is none too happy to see her, Maggie claims that she had no idea about the inheritance and warns Tommy against assuming that the money is a sure thing as she seeks his support in becoming one of the family again.

While a series of untimely miscues gives his fellow firefighters reason to suspect that Mike is gay, Sean works to help the love-struck Franco get over his failed romance as Laura struggles to put her feelings for him behind her. So, with his friends starting to outfit the station with new gym equipment and Janet pressing ahead with her plans for a lavish party to renew their vows, Tommy begins to question the sense of happiness he's been feeling. Meanwhile, as a practical joke plays on the suspicions that Mike is gay, Jerry is called home to attend to his ailing wife and is stunned to find that she's tried to commit suicide.

With Sheila finding herself on the receiving end of another vicious beating at the hands of her girlfriend, Debbie, Tommy convinces his dad to accept Maggie back into the Gavin fold. However, after a reading of the will reveals that Mrs. Ng left virtually all of her money to her beloved cats, the elder Gavin's suspicions are confirmed when Maggie suddenly bolts. Finally, as a beating from her pimp has Lou more committed than ever to save Candy from having to work as a prostitute, Tommy and Janet's world is turned upside down when their son, Connor, is killed by a hit-and-run driver.

Directed by: John Fortenberry
Written by: Denis Leary, Peter Tolan & Evan Reilly
Music: "All The Wild Horses" by Ray LaMontagne

13: JUSTICE

In the wake of his son's funeral, things for Tommy are made even more difficult when Janet holds him personally responsible for Connor being killed by a hit-and-run driver. As friends and family try to snap Tommy out of his depression, Katy's claim that she doesn't believe in God has Sean looking for a way to restore her faith. And as Jerry is told that it would be best to put his wife into the hospital, and Franco continues pressing Laura about resuming a relationship, Candy calls to tell Lou that her pimp has agreed to release her.

As Tommy fights the temptation to start drinking as a way to deal with the pain, Johnny reveals that the man who killed Connor is being returned to New York from Baltimore. After asking Johnny to alert him to when and where he will be arriving, Tommy hurries to help when Sheila calls to say that Debbie is beating her again. However, rather than seeking revenge, Tommy stands by as Debbie beats him senseless, too. Meanwhile, Sean thinks he's witnessed a miracle when a leaky church ceiling makes it look like a statue of the Virgin Mary is crying. Following his daring rescue of a girl from the ledge of a burning building, Tommy learns that Chief Perrolli has been having Mickey secretly monitor his rehab.

While Katy remains unmoved by Sean's claim of a miracle, Tommy's dad and Uncle Teddy insist on being the ones to seek revenge against Connor's killer. So, as Franco tries in vain to see Laura, and Jerry leaves his frightened wife at the hospital, Tommy agrees to let his dad and uncle shoot the hit-and-run driver when he arrives at Grand Central Station. Finally, as Lou arrives at Candy's apartment to learn that he isn't the only one who's lost a lot of money in her cleverly engineered con game, Franco finds that Laura has moved without telling him where. And after a disturbing vision of Jesus, Tommy hurries to the train station to try and stop his dad and Uncle Teddy from becoming murderers, too.

Directed by: Peter Tolan
Written by: Peter Tolan & Denis Leary
Music: "Get The Wheel" by Greg Dulli

SEASON 3

1: DEVIL

Following his son Connor's tragic death and Uncle Teddy's conviction for murdering the drunk driver who killed him, Tommy continues fighting against his own perilous downward spiral. If his ongoing battle with alcoholism wasn't enough, he must also care for his increasingly difficult father while facing Janet's determination to get a divorce. And on top of it all, when word comes down that smoking has been banned at all the city's firehouses, Jerry's challenge to see who can go the longest without a cigarette forces Tommy to forgo the one vice that he has left.

After finding condoms in her son's drawer, Sheila asks Tommy to talk to Damien. When he finally does broach the uncomfortable topic, Tommy is stunned to discover that his godson is having sex with his thirty-eight-year-old high school science teacher. But when Tommy tries to ask her to stop, Ms. Turbody refuses to discuss the matter at school as she makes it clear that she knows all about him and his problems. Meanwhile, as Jerry faces an unexpected price increase for his ailing wife's nursing home care, Lou stumbles onto a porn film starring Candy, the con artist who left him broke.

As the bet to see who can stop smoking takes its toll on everyone at 62 Truck, Tommy gets word that Janet is ready to settle their divorce. And though he's not sure how he can come up with the money, he agrees to her terms. As one by one the firefighters give in to the urge to have a cigarette, Tommy asks Teddy to make a deal with the D.A., only to discover that his uncle has no remorse for what he did. And after the news that Janet has started seeing someone else pushes him closer to the edge, Tommy finally snaps at the scene of a fire after failing to revive a young girl he tried to rescue.

Directed by: Peter Tolan

Written by: Denis Leary & Peter Tolan

Music: "Devil" by Stereophonics

2: DISCOVERY

As he and Sheila plan a birthday party for his dad, Tommy discovers that, unbeknownst to anyone else on their crew, Franco is studying for an upcoming lieutenant's exam. With the ongoing pressure of their work and home lives taking its toll, the firefighters at 62 Truck have a hard time staying true to their pledge to stop smoking. And when Jerry discreetly asks for some help to cover the increase in his wife's medical care, Lou reluctantly agrees, even though he's tapped out, too. Meanwhile, Sean tells Franco that he is secretly dating Tommy's sister, Maggie.

While out with his crew at a hot Manhattan dance club, Tommy immediately becomes the target of an overly talkative younger woman, as Mike is encouraged by some friends from his Academy class to apply for a transfer once his probation is over. While Franco is pursued by an older woman with sex on her mind, reeling under the crushing financial pressure of having been fleeced by an accomplished con artist, Lou drunkenly calls his ex-wife to ask for a family heirloom watch that he wants to sell. But when he goes to her house to steal it and is badly cut by some broken glass, Lou begins wondering if his life is even worth living anymore. Meanwhile, as Tommy learns that his daughter Colleen is now a Born Again Christian, and Jerry realizes how hard it will be to move his wife into a less expensive care facility, Sean worries about what Tommy would do if he ever found out that he is seeing Maggie.

At the Chinese restaurant where the elder Gavin has insisted his party be held, Tommy tries his best to keep his temper in check, especially after Janet shows up. However, when Tommy inadvertently spots them discreetly holding hands underneath the table, he realizes that Janet is seeing his brother Johnny. Enraged, Tommy loses his cool and unleashes a vicious assault, leaving Johnny bleeding and badly injured on the street outside.

Directed by: Peter Tolan

Written by: Peter Tolan & Denis Leary

Music: "Bonnie Brae" by Twilight Singers,
"Garota de Taquido" by Elektel,
"Say Paran" by Muddy Funksters,
"Green Grass" by Tom Quick

3: TORTURE

With Jerry's desperate pleas for money causing friction with Lou, the beating Tommy dished out after learning that his brother is seeing Janet has Sean worried about what fate has in store for him if Tommy were ever to learn that he's dating his sister, Maggie. Troubles also abound for Franco, whose older girlfriend, Alicia, isn't about to let her considerable fortune stand in the way of their relationship. As Jerry sheepishly approaches his ailing wife's estranged brother for help with her medical bills, Franco worries after seeing Lou wandering the streets drunk. Meanwhile, when Tommy demands that she stop seeing his nephew, Damien, Nell Turbody agrees—but only if he will take the teenage boy's place in her bed. And during a jailhouse visit, Tommy learns that, now that his crime has made him a celebrity behind bars, Uncle Teddy has no interest in ever getting out.

Unaware that Tommy and Franco are conspiring to torture him, Sean continues struggling to keep his relationship with Maggie under wraps. Then, after Nell calls to break things off with Damien, Sheila finds a stash of Viagra and roofies hidden in his room and asks that Tommy look into what's going on with her son. As Franco turns to Tommy with his concerns about Lou, when Tommy's refusal to acknowledge any of her calls leads him to miss picking up their daughters after school, Janet threatens to up the ante in their divorce. Meanwhile, Sean is devastated after a horse he rescued following an accident is later killed by a passing bus.

Though he comes down hard on Mike after finding him reading a popular book about Buddhist philosophy, Lou's struggle to right his own sinking ship sends him into a bookstore to steal a copy for himself. And when he realizes how much Alicia paid for the watch she gave him as a gift, Franco says that there is no way he can keep it. Finally, after Lou rebuffs Tommy's efforts to reach out to him, Jerry lands a second job at a neighborhood bar. And as Tommy urges Damien to put his relationship with Mrs. Turbody behind him, Mike seeks comfort in the arms of his roommate, Chris.

Directed by: Jace Alexander

Written by: Evan Reilly

4: SPARKS

While hurrying to the aid of a Harlem man, the crew of 62 Truck stops to help an overturned school bus full of private school students. Though the firefighters consider themselves heroes, Jerry is soon lambasted in the press for stopping to rescue the wealthy, and mostly white, children, at the expense of a black man. Unable to continue his cover-up, Sean admits that he's seeing Maggie, but is surprised to find out that Tommy has known ever since his dad's birthday party. Yet instead of being upset about their being a couple, Tommy advises that Sean get out of the relationship before Maggie does something crazy. Meanwhile, as Jerry's first day at work finds him cleaning bathrooms instead of tending bar, Sheila insists that Tommy seek out a sperm bank to ensure that the Gavins will have a male heir to work in the fire department. And despite their sexual relationship, Mike and his roommate, Chris, insist that they aren't gay.

Though Franco has a hard time finding the words, Alicia makes it clear that, despite his misgivings about their differences in age, income, and social status, she still wants a relationship with him and his daughter, Keela. While most of his friends are struggling to manage just one relationship, Tommy is simultaneously dealing with Janet, Sheila, Maggie, and Nell Turbody. And to top it all off, after agreeing to preserve the family's legacy by using a sperm bank, the sexual demands placed on Tommy leave him too exhausted to do any good.

As Sean refuses to heed Tommy's warnings about the problems that lay ahead with Maggie, Lou dismisses any suggestion that he needs to pull himself together. However, after coming within inches of suicide, he wakes Tommy in the middle of the night to ask for help. Finally, after agreeing to a face-to-face meeting with Janet to discuss their divorce, Tommy's phone conversation with Johnny reveals that the seeds of the affair between his brother and his wife were planted when they were in high school. And after his meeting with Janet sparks a violent and passionate sexual affair, Tommy leaves just seconds ahead of his angry brother's arrival.

Directed by: Jace Alexander

Written by: Denis Leary & Peter Tolan

Music: "Wild Blue Yonder" by The Screaming Blue Messiahs

5: CHLAMYDIA

As he's moving Janet out of their apartment and scheming on how to even the score with his brother, Johnny, Tommy tries setting Sean straight about the dangers of dating his sister, Maggie. After tipping Sean off to Maggie's many boyfriends, Tommy suspects he's found just the leverage he needs to make Janet and his brother squirm in Johnny's ex-wife, Angie DeCarlo. But his plans are put on hold when a panicky Sheila announces that not only has Nell Turbody been arrested for having sex with several of her high school students, but that she also gave the boys Chlamydia. Meanwhile, as Lou's financial difficulties lead to some ill-advised bets on a college basketball game, Franco worries that Alicia has kidnapped his daughter, Keela.

After promising Franco that he will help find Keela, and then worrying that he may also have contracted a venereal disease from Nell, Tommy engineers a "chance" encounter with Angie. Though she agrees to meet for a drink, once she suspects that Tommy wants to enlist her in a scheme to torment Janet and Johnny, Angie balks at cooperating. Meanwhile, as Mike's gay relationship with his roommate continues unabated and Maggie lambastes Tommy for telling Sean to dump her, Jerry's relationship with Rose blossoms. But when his brother-in-law steps up and offers to help pay for some of Jeannie's medical bills, Jerry's new affair scotches the deal.

Aware that Franco is looking for her, Alicia drops by the firehouse, telling Tommy how she's determined to spare Keela from being hurt by her dad's unhealthy relationships with women. Realizing that he's also guilty of setting a bad example for his own daughters, Tommy persuades Franco to consider allowing Keela to stay with Alicia. Finally, as Tommy finds his friendships with both Sean and Franco disintegrating, he's intrigued when Angie has a change of heart about helping with his plot to get back at Johnny and Janet.

Directed by: John Fortenberry

Written by: Evan Reilly

Music: "Shine A Light" by Wolf Parade,
"Open Heart Surgery" by Brian Jonestown Massacre

6: ZOMBIES

Following a bruising street hockey game against the Bronx Brigade that nets 62 Truck four hundred dollars, Sean patches things up with Tommy so that he can get into his stash of painkillers. As the crew argues over what to do with all the money that they have saved, and then worries after learning of a department-wide crackdown on porn at work, Sean mistakenly downs four powerful sleeping pills that are known to cause sleepwalking. Meanwhile, as being with their Uncle Johnny allows Tommy's kids to better understand the destructive effects of their dad's sarcasm and explosive temper, Teddy uses his celebrity to land himself a bride—and conjugal visits—while he's in prison.

At an abandoned warehouse that's a well-known refuge for the homeless, all but the deeply sleeping Sean head into the dilapidated building where Lou and Franco are saved from certain death by Tommy's reckless heroics. By the time the firefighters return to the station thankful that they made it out alive, Sean has already gone on a sleepwalking rampage at a nearby supermarket. Bullying his way past a cop who's been called to the scene to try and stop him, the somnambulant firefighter then heads for Maggie's apartment where he ends up cold-cocking one of her boyfriends. But when the police and the victims of his assault show up at the firehouse to complain, Sean's arrival in a stolen pet store delivery truck makes it impossible for his buddies to cover for him.

On the heels of learning that Sheila is seeing other men, Tommy heads to meet his brother's ex-wife, Angie, to carry out their plan to embarrass Johnny and Janet. Although they are hoping that an amorous public display will inspire a restaurant's gossipy host to alert Janet, she ends up telling Sheila instead. And when Janet does call asking to meet, Tommy is stunned to discover that what she wants is some rough-and-tumble sex. Finally, as Lou turns to his Uncle Red for some advice on how to deal with his problems, Mike is in the dark about his roommate Chris's affair with another man.

Directed by: John Fortenberry

Written by: Peter Tolan & Denis Leary

Music: "Numb" by Portishead,
"Brenda and Me" by Rhythm Machine

7: SATISFACTION

Having been warned in advance, the crew at 62 Truck hides their extensive collection of pornography ahead of a raid aimed at cleaning up the city's firehouses. But once the inspectors have left, the crew is stunned to discover that the almost two thousand dollars they had saved up is also gone. As Tommy uses Colleen's session with a school therapist to gain insight into his debilitating bout with survivor's guilt, Maggie says she will commit to a relationship with Sean—if he will beat up other guys in order to get her sexually aroused. And when they learn that Jerry has been spotted moonlighting at a downtown bar, Tommy and Franco pay him a visit.

Though their scheme to make Johnny and Janet jealous hasn't panned out, it has ignited a relationship between Tommy and Angie. Then, while out at a bar with his roommate, Chris, Mike is seduced by a woman who claims she can stop him from having sex with men. After learning that Jerry is having trouble getting paid by his new boss, Tommy and Franco team up to teach the deadbeat bar owner a lesson he won't soon forget. And upon making up with Maggie, Sean quickly suspects that he may not be prepared to keep her satisfied.

As Uncle Teddy begins questioning the wisdom of taking a bride while behind bars, Tommy and Angie take another stab at revenge at a police department banquet that Johnny and Janet are attending together. While Tommy finally gets under his brother's skin, Janet's reaction gives Angie reason to think twice about their childish stunt. For Johnny, he wants to get on with their new life together, but Janet can't stop thinking about ex-husband Tommy. And when Angie agrees to having a sexual relationship, Tommy has difficulty performing. Finally, as the crew suspects that Jerry donated their money to the Cancer Society and Sean gets an eyeful of mace as his reward for standing up for Maggie, Sheila spikes Tommy's food with Viagra and a powerful date rape drug to avenge his affair with Angie.

Directed by: Ken Girotti
Written by: Denis Leary & Peter Tolan
Music: "I Want To Help You Ann" by The Lyres

8: KARATE

As Tommy continues to battle his depression, he and his crew are stunned after Mike's heroic rescue leaves fellow firefighter John Stackhouse clinging to life in the hospital. Still unaware that he was drugged and raped over his relationship with Angie, Tommy apologizes to Sheila. But his problems mount when, after learning that Mike is looking to transfer to another firehouse, Tommy's breakdown at a hockey game

exposes him to a police department rival who also suffers from survivor's guilt and has turned to alcohol to cope. Meanwhile, as Jerry ends his brief affair with Rose, and Tommy begs Angie for another chance, Lou decides to get on with his life after the con artist who bankrupted him is arrested.

Though tired of constantly fighting in order to keep her interested, Sean asks Maggie to get married. And as Lou tries yoga to start turning his life around, Uncle Teddy's jailhouse wedding is undone by his fight with his bride's jealous—and murderous—ex-con former husband. Meanwhile, as Franco falls for an attractive artist he met in a bar and Mike is thrown out of the apartment by his gay roommate, Tommy is less than upbeat upon getting the news of Sean and Maggie's wedding plans.

Certain he's been given a tip on a sure thing at the racetrack, Jerry persuades his crew to pitch in on a bet that he hopes will help pay for his wife's medical bills. Even though Mike screws up when he's sent to the local OTB office, his mistake ends up picking a big winner that nets Jerry and company fifteen thousand dollars. Finally, as Franco wonders if he's falling in love with Natalie, and Sean is left to make all the plans for his wedding, Tommy persuades Angie to give him another chance. But when Janet shows up at the apartment looking for sex, in the chaos that follows, Tommy ends up losing Angie and getting beaten up by her ex-boyfriend.

Directed by: Ken Girotti
Written by: Evan Reilly
Music: "Oh Yeah" by The Subways,
"If You Love A Woman" by Dirty Pretty Things

9: PIECES

Following a fire at an indoor marijuana garden that sends the drug-addled crew of 62 Truck back to the station to sober up, a visit to the hospitalized fireman John Stackhouse leaves Tommy pondering his own future. Life for most of the other firefighters proves just as challenging when Mike's decision to move out widens a growing rift with his gay roommate, Chris, and a nurse at the hospital suggests that Jerry stop visiting his ailing wife in order to maintain his own sanity. And as Franco wonders what secrets his new girlfriend is keeping from him, Sean claims that marrying Maggie will make him a member of the Gavin clan.

Lou's buying a motorcycle and considering leaving the department to join a cousin on his fishing boat in Florida and Franco's preparing for the upcoming lieutenant's exam has Tommy worrying about what will happen to him if the crew he trusts with his life breaks up. So, as Sean seeks Maggie's dad's blessing for their marriage, Sheila looks to ease Tommy's fears by offering to marry him so he can retire on the millions of dollars she received as a result of her husband's death at the World Trade Center. Meanwhile, now that he's married, Uncle Teddy finds that the much-touted conjugal visits aren't as much fun as he had hoped.

As Tommy considers Sheila's offer, things at the firehouse become even tenser when, in the wake of Chris' visit, the firefighters discover that Mike has been living with a gay man. But while his partners are virtually unanimous in their revulsion, Tommy surprises everyone by jumping to Mike's defense. Finally, as Franco learns that Natalie isn't living with another boyfriend, but is actually caring for her mentally ill brother, Tommy gets word that Janet and Johnny are expecting a baby.

Directed by: Jace Alexander

Written by: Peter Tolan & Denis Leary

10: RETARDS

As Tommy continues his grim bedside vigil for John Stackhouse, he asks to see Janet, especially now that she's having a baby that could either be his or Johnny's. While Tommy's spirits are lifted by the new Cadillac Sheila has offered in exchange for giving his old truck to Damien, the joy is short-lived when it's stolen. As the merciless ribbing about his sex life prompts Mike to demand a transfer, Tommy's fears about the crew breaking up appear to be coming true. Meanwhile, Franco looks to score points by bringing Natalie's mentally challenged brother, Richard, to work.

When he sees a truck that looks like the one he just lost, Tommy berates his Arab cab driver into trying to follow it before being dropped off at Janet's. Walking in on their violent standoff, Johnny orders Tommy to leave—and never come back. And when confronted by Jimmy's ghost, Tommy is surprised when he tells him to marry Sheila. Meanwhile, a woman from the nursing home asks Jerry out on a date.

After managing to torpedo Mike's transfer, the near-pen-niless Tommy gets drunk on some pricey Irish whiskey at a bar where he unleashes his anger and frustration before being rescued by Mickey. Back at the firehouse, Franco jeopardizes his relationship with Natalie when, after asking Mike and Sean to watch Richard, they lose him. Finally, as Tommy's dad criticizes him for not being able to hold his life together, Sean worries that Maggie isn't taking their upcoming wedding seriously. And as Jerry finds himself on a date with Karlene, Tommy is both sad and relieved when Stackhouse dies.

Directed by: Jace Alexander

Written by: Evan Reilly

11: TWILIGHT

Following a pair of tense rescues of a wheelchair-bound quadriplegic and an obese woman impaled on an iron fence, Tommy wakes up to face another day to find that his dad has nearly set the kitchen on fire. After Tommy suggests that his dad might be safer in a nursing home, he gets another big surprise when Lou admits to spending the night with a nun. But Tommy's problems only get worse when Sheila calls to say that his dad has disappeared after leaving a suicide note. Meanwhile, as Franco suspects that Natalie's brother may be faking his mental illness, and Sean asks Maggie to agree to a church wedding, Jerry suffers from performance anxiety when Karlene suggests having sex.

While searching for the elder Gavin, Lou is suspicious when Tommy says he's OK with his retiring to work on his cousin's fishing boat. Then, after a thorough search of a host of Irish bars doesn't produce a lead, Tommy finds his dad at the cemetery where his wife, Mary, nephew Jimmy and grandson Connor are buried. And after convincing his dad that he won't send him away, Tommy is intrigued when Lou suggests that the old man move in with his aging Uncle Red. Meanwhile, as Franco gets Richard to admit to his ruse, Sean is upset after Maggie's rude behavior causes a priest to refuse to marry them in the church.

When Jerry wants some Viagra before his next date with Karlene, Tommy asks to Sheila to help, unaware that she's about to buy a beach house where they can live together. While Sean tells Maggie that he is calling off their engagement, Mike looks to curb his homosexual impulses by spending the night with Paula. Finally, as Tommy and

Lou realize that pairing up the two old men in their lives may just work, and Jerry's next date with Karlene ends in disaster when he dies during sex, Johnny is cut down in the line of duty by a trio of gunshots.

Directed by: John Fortenberry

Written by: John Scurti

12: HELL

As Tommy breaks the tragic news of Johnny's death, he's surprised when their dad insists on a funeral that celebrates his late son's life rather than one that mourns his passing. Tommy feels like he dodged a bullet after hearing his dad's reaction. But upon learning that Jerry had a near-fatal stroke during sex, he turns around and blames himself for giving him the Viagra that caused the disaster. And despite hearing phone messages Johnny left before being killed that clearly indicate an approaching reconciliation with his brother, Tommy cannot bring himself to exact revenge on his killer even when given the opportunity.

As Ellie's reaction to the news about Johnny leads Uncle Teddy to conclude that he doesn't want to be married, Natalie suspects that Franco's interest in her is due to her uncanny resemblance to his daughter. When Jerry's son, Peter, arrives at the hospital, Mike peppers him with questions about being gay. And as Mike is exploring the possibility that he's bisexual, Sean learns that Maggie never wants to see him again. Meanwhile, as Lou is overjoyed when the nun he's been sleeping with says she's ready to leave the church and join him on his cousin's boat, an emotional phone message left for Johnny helps Janet realize that Tommy still loves her.

As the arrival of the Gavins' estranged sister, Rosemarie, surprises everyone at Johnny's funeral, Maggie changes her mind and offers to marry Sean if they do it right there in the cemetery. Then, back at his apartment, Tommy discovers just how much his advice on life meant to Rosemarie. And after promising to take care of Janet now that Johnny is gone, Tommy decides to leave the department when Sheila says that she bought the beach house he liked.

Directed by: Peter Tolan

Written by: Denis Leary & Peter Tolan

Music: "Hell Is Around The Corner" by Tricky

13: BEACHED

The days following his brother's funeral and his sister's wedding find Tommy wrestling with his promises to care for Janet and their kids now that Johnny is dead, and to retire to the beachfront home Sheila has bought for them to start life anew. As Jerry's stroke leads to the appointment of a temporary replacement, Franco enlists Natalie's brother to help him prepare for the lieutenant's exam and Mike considers a ménage à trois with a brother and sister. And as Maggie and Sean are caught having sex on the new chief's desk, Lou tricks Tommy into having dinner with Theresa, the nun whom he is planning to live with on board his cousin's fishing boat.

As Tommy soon discovers, the difficulty keeping his promise to care for their kids pales in comparison to what he and Janet are up against when they have to come up with an explanation for her pregnancy. In the wake of his date with Sara and Greg, Mike reconsiders any thoughts of his suspected bisexuality, and things suddenly become even more complicated when Jerry escapes from the hospital and shows up at work. Meanwhile, as failing to complete the lieutenant's exam leads Franco to realize that he isn't really prepared to care for his daughter, a visit to the fishing boat with Theresa convinces Lou that he isn't cut out for life on the water.

Though he hasn't said anything about it at work, Tommy goes to file his retirement papers but balks before he's done. Meeting face-to-face to tell Keela that she is better off living with Alicia, Franco learns that she's being sent to a boarding school in Europe. Finally, as Lou tells Theresa that he cannot live on a boat, and Maggie insists on having sex at the firehouse, Tommy's friends change their minds about leaving 62 Truck. And once Tommy reveals that he has to take care of Janet and the kids, an angry Sheila drugs him into unconsciousness during their first beach house dinner and then leaves in a panic after accidentally starting a fire.

Directed by: Peter Tolan

Written by: Peter Tolan & Denis Leary

Music: "The One I Love" by David Gray

SEASON 4

1: BABYFACE

In the wake of the fire that nearly killed him and destroyed the Long Island beachfront home, Tommy is questioned by arson investigators about a pair of insurance policies that he doesn't remember signing—one on the house and one on Sheila. His future in serious jeopardy, Tommy struggles to care for Janet, her new baby, and their two daughters, a task made more difficult now that Colleen is drinking, smoking pot, and dating a 26-year-old musician. As his incessant crying has Janet worried about whether the baby likes her and Tommy wondering about the father's identity, Jerry looks to get his life back on track following his stroke and Franco tries to keep things with Natalie moving forward, while Sean tries to convince Maggie to set aside her fascination with pornography.

With Cousin Eddie working to find out anything he can about the arson investigation, Chief Pecher reveals that the NYFD brass are looking to dump Tommy to avoid the bad publicity that a trial would bring. And while Tommy is upset to learn that Lou has decided to install a basketball court at the firehouse instead of the hockey rink they had agreed on, Jerry's gay son Peter asks him to be the best man at his upcoming wedding.

After fielding a frustrated call from Janet looking for help with the crying baby, Tommy and the crew arrive at a fire where their effort to save some trapped cats nearly kills them all as the building collapses. As Jerry dictates a compromise on the gym that pleases no one, Tommy is uncomfortable with being pursued by Nona Ovitz, the female Long Island volunteer firefighter who pulled him out of the burning beach house. But after Tommy reluctantly agrees to a date with Nona, Sheila warns him against doing anything that might jeopardize their insurance scam.

Directed by: Peter Tolan
Written by: Denis Leary & Peter Tolan
Music: "Dance This Mess Around" by B-52's,
"Backseat Nothing" by The Del Fuegos

2: TUESDAY

Accused of an arson fire that he can't explain, Tommy turns to Sheila for answers. While Sheila tries to claim that his memory was clouded by his drinking, when pressed for details he can give to the police, she admits that the fire started after Tommy flew into a rage over his sudden impotence. Though Tommy is uncomfortable with the plan, Eddie is certain that the explanation will satisfy the arson investigators. Meanwhile, as Lou looks to rebuild the firehouse's basketball team by recruiting an athletic rookie firefighter, and Franco keeps Richie from being arrested for making a scene at a jewelry store, Maggie tells Sean that she has decided to give up her porn collection. And now that he's sure that he's about to be cleared to return to work, Jerry begins reasserting his authority at 62 Truck.

While Tony's legal troubles remain unresolved, the jury returns a not guilty verdict in Uncle Teddy's manslaughter case. As Tommy and Eddie look to help Teddy and his new bride, Ellie, get settled now that he's out of jail, Janet calls to say that Colleen has run away with her boyfriend. So, as Tommy puts off his date with Nona so he can search for Colleen, and Mike refuses to leave his dying mother alone at the hospital, Teddy uses a restaurant's bathroom window to escape a life with Ellie.

Still worried that Maggie is thinking about other men even though she's thrown out her porn collection, Sean questions his friends about their sexual fantasies and accidentally lets it slip that one of his is about Tommy's wife, Janet. Finally, when Sheila calls to say that her interview with the arson investigators went well and that she is dating the firefighter who pulled her from the burning house, Tommy calls to confirm his date with Nona. And once he gets word of Colleen's whereabouts, he enlists the crew of 62 Truck to help retrieve her.

Directed by: Jace Alexander
Written by: Peter Tolan & Denis Leary
Music: "Wolf Like Me" by TV On The Radio

3: COMMITMENT

After dragging the crew of 62 Truck to the apartment where Colleen is living with her boyfriend, Tommy makes it painfully clear that Tony should steer clear of his daughter. But the approach backfires, and Janet chastises Tommy and orders him to apologize. As Jerry learns that his stroke has left him facing a desk job, Mike refuses to believe that there's nothing more that can be done about his mom's cancer. But the greatest shock comes when his mother asks him to help her die. To cope with his grief, Mike turns to Tommy. And though Tommy tries to steer clear of Mike, he is forced to reconsider after Nona continues pestering him about a date.

As Tommy tries avoiding dinner with Mike or Nona, and Sheila realizes that she isn't all that interested in a relationship with the firefighter who saved her life, Jerry announces that he is taking a job at headquarters. Seeing it as an opportunity to save his own career, Tommy asks him to help torpedo the arson investigation. After Mike finally talks him into going out for dinner, and then seeks his advice on how to handle his mother's request, Tommy tells him that this is his last chance to do right by his mom and suggests using an overdose of morphine. Things get even more uncomfortable for Tommy when he realizes that it looks like he and Mike are on a date. So once Nona shows up to ambush him, Tommy accepts a ride home and then excuses himself for the night, but only after agreeing to another date.

Following his release from jail, Uncle Teddy seeks refuge at the home of his former prison guard. As Lenny reluctantly agrees to let Uncle Teddy stay, and Jerry gets a set of golf clubs as a going-away gift from 62 Truck, Tommy's plan to regain Colleen's respect by letting Tony beat him up has exactly the opposite effect. Finally, as Mike realizes that the nurse did his dirty work for him by killing his mom before he could, Jerry's depression over having to finish his career behind a desk leads him to commit suicide.

Directed by: Jace Alexander

Written by: Evan Reilly

Music: "Last Goodbye" by Adam Roth

4: PUSSIFIED

While the funeral for Mike's mom is getting underway, Tommy learns of Jerry's suicide. To see that nothing disrupts the benefits that the late Chief's son deserves, Tommy persuades the medical examiner to rule the death a heart attack. Finding Uncle Teddy hiding out at the house

of his former prison guard, Ellie insists that he enter rehab for his alcoholism. However, making it clear that his real problem is his fear of being on the outside, Teddy isn't so sure that he wants any help. Meanwhile, as Tommy agrees to buy Colleen some furniture for her and Tony's apartment in exchange for keeping in touch with him and Janet, Nona drops by the station house to make sure that he won't back out on their upcoming date. But when she and Tommy are out on the following night, it's clear that he is having sexual performance problems.

Seeing Tommy trying hard to be a better parent prompts Janet to suggest they see a marriage counselor to try and repair their marriage. As Sheila brings news that the insurance company has agreed to pay her claim for the burned beach house, Sean threatens to get a divorce in order to get Maggie to stop drinking, but is stunned when she agrees to end their marriage. Following a fire where he helps deliver a baby inside a burning building, Tommy joins Janet at the counselor's office. But once the counselor hears the sordid details of their history together, he suggests they see someone else for help.

As Lou uses blackmail in order to recruit an athletic young rookie to revitalize the station house's basketball team, Franco buys Natalie an expensive engagement ring, only to get cold feet before he can pop the question. While Tommy encourages Franco to go through with it, breaking up with Maggie prompts Sean to ask if he can stay with Mike. Finally, when Janet tries interesting Tommy in sex, not only is she surprised to discover that he can't perform, but that he has been having the same problem with another woman.

Directed by: Jace Alexander

Written by: Denis Leary & Peter Tolan

Music: "Dayton Ohio 1903" by Randy Newman

5: BLACK

As he and his colleagues are recovering from Jerry's suicide and welcoming their new chief, Sidney Feinberg, Tommy calls Nona to say that he's ready for their long-promised date. As Tommy looks forward to having sex again, and Teddy checks into rehab to deal with his alcoholism, Sean's hopes for saving his failing marriage are dashed after he comes home to find Maggie with another man. Meanwhile, as Lou tries to get Theresa to cut back on sex, and Franco proposes to Natalie, Mike refuses to allow Sean to be in his house alone.

During the next hockey game against their rivals in the police department, everyone sees that Tommy's skills on the rink aren't anywhere near what they used to be. Although their coach mercifully benches Tommy for Mike, Sheila's boyfriend, Troy, insists that Gavin is only faking it in an effort to draw the cops into a trap. As Sheila demands that Troy keep quiet, especially once Mike picks up the slack against the cops, Lou asks Franco to help recruit a rookie firefighter that he has targeted to revive 62 Truck's basketball team. Meanwhile, as Uncle Teddy balks after realizing that he is expected to actually quit drinking, and Sheila offers Tommy $400,000 from her insurance settlement, Lou talks Theresa into a moratorium on sex.

Although Nona reveals that Tommy was actually able to perform sexually on the night that the beach house burned down, she decides that dating him is just too difficult. As Teddy looks to stay on the lam from the rehab center, Lou and Franco set out to convince the basketball-playing rookie, Bart, to join 62 Truck. But to get him to cooperate, Lou not only agrees that he won't have to perform the normal rookie chores, but that everyone can call him Shawn. Finally, Tommy realizes that Janet has lost all interest in being a mother to her new baby.

Directed by: Jace Alexander

Written by: Mike Martineau

Music: "Tell Me What You Want" by The Black Hollies

6: BALANCE

While Tommy is shocked at the degree to which Lou acquiesced in order to get Bart—a.k.a. Shawn—to agree to join 62 Truck, Sean is placed in the delicate position of having to come up with a new name. As Sean's search produces some all-too-predictable sarcasm from the crew, and Tommy continues to come under pressure to let Sheila raise Janet's new baby, Uncle Teddy's move to a new rehab facility is as unsuccessful as his last one. Meanwhile, as Mike goes out of his way to keep Sean out of his late mother's bedroom, Tommy discovers that the new chief is much more interested in basketball than hockey. And when Chief

Feinberg suggests having a scrimmage, Tommy's ineptitude at basketball is exposed for all to see.

As a phone call from his daughter's new stepmother, Alicia, has Natalie questioning Franco's fidelity, Teddy escapes from another rehab clinic. And when Tommy notices that Janet's son isn't universally loved at home, Sheila is stunned to find that her boyfriend, Troy, has erected a shrine to Tommy Gavin at his apartment. Meanwhile, obsessed with finding out what Mike is hiding in his late mother's bedroom, Sean turns to his crewmates for help in uncovering the truth.

When confronted by Tommy about what happened on the night of the fire, Sheila continues to stick to her story that his rage over his inability to perform in bed precipitated the accident. Finally, as Tommy buys Colleen and Tony a new bed for their apartment, Lou is outraged after uncovering evidence that Teresa is having an affair with Cousin Mike. And when Sean discovers photos that suggest Mike's parents were gay, he accidentally sets a fire that burns down the house.

Directed by: Don Scardino

Written by: Evan Reilly

Music: "Wedding Song" by Abel

7: SEVEN

Upon arriving at the scene of an apartment house fire, the crew of 62 Truck immediately sets to work trying to save the trapped occupants, only to watch helplessly as children are desperately thrown from the burning windows to their deaths on the street below. Although the crew considers their efforts to be heroic, the media coverage of the blaze and the loss of life are harsh. As a result, Troy loses all respect for Tommy, dismantling his shrine to him and cutting off all contact with Sheila. Meanwhile, Franco's resolve to marry Natalie is tested when Alicia returns from Europe and suggests getting back together to raise his daughter, Keela.

As Black Shawn leads the newly reconstituted firehouse basketball team to another victory, Colleen calls Tommy to ask for money, while Sheila phones to say that Troy has left her in the wake of what's being called "the baby fire." While he broaches the subject of Sheila's offer to take Janet's baby, Tommy still can't bring himself to agree to the deal he's been offered. And in the wake of the basketball game, Lou discourages Theresa from continuing their relationship by saying that he wants to have children.

Tommy's problems continue to mount as Mickey reveals that, in addition to receiving a call from Maggie asking for help with her drinking, Uncle Teddy's wife called to say that he needs help, too. And as Mike tells Sean the truth about how he started the fire that burned down his mom's house, Franco has second thoughts about marrying Natalie. Finally, as Lou looks to put Theresa behind him once and for all, Johnny's ghost tries to convince Tommy to throw the baby off a bridge.

Directed by: Don Scardino

Written by: Peter Tolan & Denis Leary

Music: "The Lure Would Prove Too Much" by The Twilight Singers, "Some Unholy War" by Amy Winehouse

8: SOLO

After considering all the options, including throwing Janet's baby off a bridge, Tommy accepts Sheila's offer. Despite the difficulties Janet had while raising the child, the news that the baby is gone causes her to lash out, telling Tommy that she and Katy are leaving him for good— but not before trying to run him down with her car. Calling in sick, Tommy is then forced to wrestle with his own demons in a frightening dream in which he is confronted by the ghosts of Jimmy and Johnny. Meanwhile, as the crew speculates about the real reason that Tommy didn't show up for his shift, a traffic accident en route from a fire injures Mike's knee.

As Mike settles into a new apartment and Sean decides to give Maggie one last chance, Janet stalks Sheila and her little boy. Now that Tommy is on his own, Chief Feinberg presses him to go out on a date with his daughter, Beth. And while Franco hopes to spend the night with Alicia even after telling her that he isn't cut out for marriage, she refuses to be used and forces him to admit that he really loves Natalie.

As Lou turns to drinking with Cousin Mike in an effort to forget Theresa, and Mickey arranges an intervention aimed at stopping Maggie and Uncle Teddy's drinking, Tommy agrees to a dinner date with Beth. Realizing that he really has his hands full with her, Tommy uses his cell phone

to sneak a call to Lou asking for help escaping from his date. But before has to rely on his friend to bail him out, Tommy gets a lucky break when a fire at a building across the street sends him running to the rescue.

Directed by: Ken Girotti

Written by: Denis Leary & Peter Tolan & Evan Reilly

Music: "Running" by Adam Roth

9: ANIMAL

Now that he's laid up with a knee injury, Mike can't get anyone to keep him company at home. While Franco is spending his spare time with Black Shawn, Sean and Tommy are at an intervention for Maggie and Uncle Teddy. As the gathering brings out all the Gavin family's worst traits, Ellie chooses to stay mum until she's had a chance to deliver her comments to Teddy in person, while Sean comes with several notebooks full of things he wants Maggie to hear. But when Sean is deprived of the opportunity once Maggie quickly agrees to go to rehab, and Teddy insists that he can't go back into a facility, the Gavins decide to organize their own A.A. meetings. Meanwhile, as news that he had been seeing Alicia prompts Natalie to break things off with Franco, Tommy rents a shabby apartment where he can start putting his life back together.

At the John Gavin Memorial Scholarship Fund Hockey Game, Tommy surprises everyone by playing for the police department. Yet, after leading the cops to victory, he accepts an offer to rejoin the fire department team. And after calling a phone number that was slipped into his pocket on the night he was out with Chief Feinberg's daughter, Beth, Tommy ends up in an intense, albeit brief, sexual encounter with a woman he barely knows.

As Mike contemplates suicide, Sheila turns to Tommy when Katy and Janet kidnap the baby. After Chief Feinberg takes him to task for not calling Beth, Tommy senses that his life is crumbling around him and risks his life to save the occupants of a burning building. Finally, upon failing to get Janet to return the baby, Tommy finds Mike in the aftermath of his half-hearted suicide attempts. But when Tommy tries to make a point by pretending to kill himself, he's left dangling when the fire escape on Mike's building suddenly collapses.

Directed by: Ken Girotti

Written by: Evan Reilly

Music: "Swing Low" by Rocco DeLuca & The Burden

10: HIGH

As Tommy promises Colleen a new car in exchange for information on Janet's love life and secretly allowing Sheila access to the baby for two days each week, Lou looks to get revenge for Theresa's indiscretions with Cousin Mike. While pondering sleeping with the waitress Mike is currently dating, he counsels Tommy to placate Chief Feinberg by going out on another date with his daughter, Beth. Facing personal problems of his own, Franco enlists Natalie's brother, Richie, to find out who she's seeing in the wake of their recent breakup.

With Black Shawn and Chief Feinberg complaining of rampant racism within the fire department, Colleen leads Tommy to the real estate office where Janet is working while dating her handsome boss. Just when Tommy is on the verge of drinking again to cope with his mounting problems, Mickey heads him off outside a neighborhood bar. Then, after doing his best to help Mike with the depression that's resulted from his knee injury, Tommy tries to deflect the sexual advances of the nameless woman who's been pursuing him.

With his life spinning out of control, Tommy is summoned to a bar where his dad is facing down his own drinking problem. After learning that, as a boy, he was deathly afraid of heights, Tommy takes refuge in a nearby church, where he's accidentally mistaken for a priest. Finally, as Sean decides to become an alcoholic in order to better understand Maggie, and Mike gets an unexpected surprise after being picked up at a bar by a beautiful older woman, Tommy's fear of heights is brought into focus as he rescues a window washer trapped thirty-five floors above the street.

Directed by: John Fortenberry

Written by: Peter Tolan & Denis Leary

11: CYCLE

As he's dealing with nightmares about the deaths of his friends and persistent requests for sex from the anonymous woman he saved from a fire while out with Beth Feinberg, Tommy makes a legally questionable deal to get Colleen the car he promised in exchange for access to Janet's baby. Faced with Colleen's pointed questions about how their failed marriage has damaged the family, Tommy tries to defend how he and Janet raised her and her siblings. And after cautiously placing the baby in Sheila's care for the next couple of days, he finally learns the name of the woman who's been pursuing him, only to discover that her history dictates that their fledgling relationship is doomed.

Now that he has decided to match Maggie drink-for-drink as a way to better understand her, Sean is determined to prove to himself and his skeptical colleagues that he is an alcoholic, too. As Tommy proposes using a street hockey game to teach Black Shawn an important lesson, the next Gavin family rehab meeting disintegrates in rancor after Mickey asks everyone to apologize to those they have hurt over the years. And after his dad tries apologizing for his own mistakes as a parent, Tommy's efforts to get back into Chief Feinberg's good graces by taking Beth out again backfire.

At the street hockey game, Black Shawn's inexperience gets him off to a rocky start until some tips from Garrity and Mike help turn things around. Finally, after being forced to take the wheel of the fire truck for a call that comes in during a birthday party at work, Tommy insists on remaining anonymous after helping the drunken firefighters rescue the building's occupants.

Directed by: John Fortenberry

Written by: John Scurti

Music: "Act Nice and Gentle" by The Black Keys

12: KEEFE

When Mike is transferred to a new crew with a reputation for drinking on the job, Tommy decides to take some measures to keep the former probie out of trouble. After secretly slipping into the firehouse, he dons the bunker jacket that once belonged to his late cousin, Jimmy, and then hides on the truck to join Mike and his crew. Meanwhile, as Lou discovers that ending his relationship with Cousin Mike's lusty girlfriend is going to be harder than he thought, Natalie confronts Franco about using her brother to spy on her, but still leaves the door open for reconciliation.

After complaining to Val that their relationship is about nothing other than sex, Tommy gets a call from the bank regarding some charges on the credit card he gave Colleen. While Colleen admits to using the card to pay for her boyfriend's time in a recording studio, Tommy points out that he also used it to buy an expensive diamond engagement ring. And when Tommy confronts him, Tony admits that he bought it for the girl he is planning to marry—not for Colleen. Meanwhile, after Lou and Cousin Mike put his alleged alcoholism to the test, Sean is shocked to wake up the following morning in bed with an unattractive woman. And though a night out with Black Shawn lands Franco in bed with a beautiful girl, it also helps him see how much he misses Natalie.

Continuing to sneak off on calls with Mike's crew, Tommy manages to save the hard-drinking firefighters from making a fatal mistake. And though Tommy carefully avoids being recognized, some of the firefighters are certain that they saw Jimmy Keefe's ghost. Finally, despite the fact Tommy saved her from a doomed relationship, Colleen is still angry that he interfered. And while Chief Feinberg is upset over his conduct with Beth, Tommy has sex with a woman as he is saving her from a burning building.

Directed by Jace Alexander

Written by Denis Leary & Peter Tolan & Evan Reilly

Music: "New York" by Superthriller,
"100 Days" by Mark Lanegan

13: YAZ

With Tommy continuing to battle his alcoholism while secretly living in a 62 Truck storeroom, his fellow firefighters are spooked by sightings of the late Jimmy Keefe. While Chief Feinberg has had his fill of the ghost stories, he's unaware that what his men have actually seen is Tommy in disguise. Meanwhile, as Franco learns that Natalie is in Chicago with her new boyfriend, and Colleen is throwing Tony out of their apartment, Sheila continues pressing Tommy for more time alone with Janet's baby.

As Tommy tries to understand why his marriage failed, new girlfriend Valerie makes it clear that she is looking for a purely sexual relationship on her own terms. Struggling with her own twin addictions to booze and sex, Maggie calls on personal experience to explain to Sean that he doesn't have

what it takes to be an alcoholic. And though he's troubled to learn that Latrina has been sleeping with Lou, Cousin Mike is really upset to discover that his new girlfriend has also been showering him with edible delicacies. Meanwhile, Sheila takes Tommy to task for not telling her about the sightings of her late husband.

As Tommy decides to give Valerie what she's craving, Colleen finds a sympathetic ear in Black Shawn when she blames her dad for coming between her and Tony. Finally, as Franco tells Natalie that he's willing to give her time to make up her mind about their future together, Sheila takes advantage of Tommy's trip to a baseball game with his dad and Uncle Teddy to take a look inside the storage closet where he is staying. And as Sheila discovers that he's been masquerading as Jimmy, Tommy's dad dies at the ballpark.

Directed by Jace Alexander

Written by Peter Tolan & Denis Leary & Evan Reilly

Music: "My Drug Buddy" by The Lemonheads,
"Good Times Roll" by The Cars

The Leary Firefighters Foundation was founded in 2000 by actor Denis Leary in response to a fire that broke out in an abandoned warehouse in downtown Worcester, Massachusetts, his hometown, in December of 1999. Over 75 firefighters ran into what some have called "the perfect fire" and six of them never came out. One was Denis' first cousin, Jerry Lucey, and another, Lt. Tommy Spencer, was a childhood friend and high school classmate. In an effort to find a positive way to deal with this overwhelming loss, Denis established The Leary Firefighters Foundation in the spring of 2000. The Foundation is dedicated to providing fire departments with funding and resources for up-to-date equipment and training.

A lifelong hockey fan, Denis teamed up with Boston Bruins legends Bobby Orr and Cam Neely to organize The Celebrity Hat Trick, "Hockey's Greatest Skate for America's Bravest," a two-day event that features two teams made up of hockey legends and Hollywood celebrities. Funds raised from these events have been used to build a new burn tower and training facility and to purchase a new rescue boat and an SCBA Response Unit, a mobile maintenance unit to service and repair air tanks.

On August 11, 2004, the Boston Fire Department, a Tactical Command Unit, was presented with a retro-fitted Ford Excursion SUV, an emergency management vehicle capable of increased communications control and improved maneuverability on Boston's narrow streets. Other funds have been directed towards the equipment needs of the Boston Fire Department, including the Tactical Command Unit and the acquisition of a new Fire Rescue / Diver Support Boat for the Department's protection of Boston Harbor.

In the wake September 11, 2001, The Leary Firefighters Foundation established The Fund for New York's Bravest to raise money for the families of the 343 firefighters who perished in the line of duty. With enormous support from friends in the entertainment community, the LFF threw a landmark New York City benefit, The BASH for New York's Bravest, and raised over $1.9 million before it closed in 2003. Every dollar collected went directly into the hands of the families, without any administrative costs. The BASH for New York's Bravest is now an annual, celebrity-studded event that continues to honor New York's firefighters while raising funds to support their equipment and training needs.

In 2002, the LFF expanded their focus to include assisting the FDNY with their critical need to enhance operations and advance first responder training. An in-depth working relationship has been formed with senior commanders and it is through their expertise that the LFF prioritizes the disbursement of funds received from donors. Using dollars raised at The 2003 BASH for New York's Bravest, the LFF partnered with the FDNY's Fire Safety Education Fund to purchase a Mobile Command Center for the FDNY. This emergency management vehicle, which was deployed on July 19, 2004, is equipped with state-of-the-art audio and video monitoring capabilities and directly answers the call for a heightened level of communications and planning at large-scale events and emergencies. It serves as a visible point of contact for communications between the FDNY, NYPD, FBI and OEM, as well as media and local officials, and as a staging area at major events. The LFF has also donated two Flashover Simulators to the FDNY Fire Academy on Randall's Island that were incorporated into the

training regimen of both probationary and veteran firefighters.

Every community relies on their firefighters to keep their population safe. Their bravery and commitment to saving lives is indisputable and is demonstrated on a daily basis. The LFF current development campaign is focused on two major projects: building a technologically advanced High-Rise Simulator at the FDNY Fire Academy to improve training to combat the potentially catastrophic high-rise fire and ensuring funding for the completion of the Worcester training facility, including construction of a second building that will feature a state-of-the-art Emergency Operations Center (a first for Central Massachusetts) and a physical training facility.

The Leary Firefighters Foundation remains dedicated to keeping the needs of firefighters in the forefront of the country's awareness and to upholding our pledge to provide them with funding and resources to acquire the tools necessary to maintain the highest level of public safety.

Leary Firefighters Foundation
594 Broadway, Suite 409
New York, NY 10012
212.343.0240
info@learyfirefighters.org
www.learyfirefightersfoundation.org

ACKNOWLEDGMENTS

We wish to thank the following for their special contributions to the book:

At Apostle Productions: Denis Leary, Peter Tolan, Jim Serpico, Tom Sellitti, Evan Reilly, and Anna Urban.

At Sony Pictures Television: Karen Barragan, Jeanie Bradley, AnneMarie Carretta, Debra Curtis, Alan Daniels, Jamie Erlicht, Mike Freeman, Steve Mosko, Robert Oswaks, Karina Payton, Karen Tatevosian, and Zack Van Amburg.

At Sony Pictures Consumer Products: George Leon, Greg Economos, Mark Caplan, and Cindy Irwin.

At FX Networks: Sally Daws, Stephanie Gibbons, Todd Heughens, John Landgraf, Kenna McCabe, John Solberg, and John Varvi.

At Chop Shop Music Supervision: Alexandra Patsavas and Kasey Truman.

Special thanks to project editor Linda Sunshine and to Tim Shaner at Night and Day Design (nightanddaydesign.biz).

Also, to the Newmarket team, including Frank DeMaio, Paul Sugarman, Linda Carbone, Heidi Sachner, Harry Burton, and Tracey Bussell.

—Esther Margolis, Publisher, and Keith Hollaman, Executive Editor, Newmarket Press